BIG BAND DRUMMING

Fill-osophy

STEVE FIDYK & DAVE BLACK

Tempo Change Software

The MP3 CD includes instrument specific demonstration recordings and play-along accompaniments. These MP3 files can be played with the included tempo change software, uploaded easily to your MP3 player or transferred to your computer. This application requires Quicktime (7.6.7 or higher), and Java (7.6.7 or higher) to be installed on your computer.

Produced by
Alfred Music
P.O. Box 10003
Van Nuys, CA 91410-0003
alfred.com

Printed in USA.

ISBN-10: 1-4706-1005-1
ISBN-13: 978-1-4706-1005-0

Table of Contents

Introduction

Welcome to *Big Band Drumming Fill-osophy*. This book contains drum fills in a variety of musical styles as applied to a specific idiom—big band jazz.

Big band drum fills are improvised rhythms that help prepare or **set up** specific entrances within a composition, adding excitement and variety to an arrangement. Musical drum fills are influenced in part by the tempo, dynamics, and musical style of the composition.

Big band drum fills:

- are played with a consistent pulse.

- are clear and purposeful.

- match the context of the arrangement (for example, swing, funk, or Latin vocabulary).

- are **understandable** to the musicians you're accompanying.

- can be **under-** or **overstated** to add excitement to the composition.

- are played with a sense of **dynamics** (for example, a phrase that crescendos from *piano* to *forte*).

- are an example of one's creativity.

They also serve specific functions within an arrangement, such as:

- helping to **delineate** the form of the musical composition.

- **leading** an ensemble into or out of phrases.

- providing **cohesion** when played in between phrases that contain ensemble or section figures.

- **bonding** sections of an arrangement together (for example, the introduction, melody, solo sections, shout chorus, restatement of the melody, and coda).

The book is divided into two sections:

> **Part 1** introduces **primer fill examples** and includes section and ensemble phrases to practice fill vocabulary in swing, funk, and Latin styles. Ensemble examples are highlighted with an "instrumental target point," so you can clearly see how the drum fill functions and where it leads.

> **Part 2** provides fills *in context*, extracted from big band arrangements of varying styles. As you practice these examples, we suggest you use the slow-down software provided on the MP3 CD. Begin each extracted fill "under tempo" and gradually increase the speed until you have control of each rhythm at the desired tempo.

Big Band Drumming Fill-osophy has been written with the assumption that you already have a basic understanding of music notation and drumset coordination. If lacking in these areas, we recommend first completing the study of an introductory snare drum or drumset method. If you have any questions regarding notation, go back to the beginning method, and review it before reading the enclosed drum parts.

About the MP3 CD

The book includes a professional-quality MP3 CD with full-band tracks in a variety of musical styles (Latin, swing, funk, etc.). Many of the written examples from Part 1 are performed on the accompanying CD so you can hear the drum sound, dynamic balance, and rhythmic flow of each drum fill. In addition, the CD contains "phrases (minus drums)," featuring a professional big band. We've included these phrases to help simulate a live performance situation for practicing the written fills in Part 1. The excerpts from Part 2 contain "fills in context (with drums)." We recommend that you first listen to the track and read the short analysis contained in the book to gain an understanding of the interpretation and style for each.

Acknowledgments

Steve Fidyk would like to thank Dave Black and Pete BarenBregge at Alfred Music for their support and the opportunity to share my teaching ideas and experience. To my parents, John and Loretta Fidyk, for believing in me and for encouraging music as a profession. To my teachers, Angele Stella, Bob Nowak, Ed Soph, Joe Morello, Kim Plainfield, and John Riley, for the musical and technical tools. A very special thanks to my son, Tony, for his help with this book (especially the *Fill-inspiration Selected Discography*), and to my wife Tamela and son Joey for their guidance, patience, and love.

Dave Black would like to thank Steve Fidyk and Raj Mallikarjuna for their invaluable input and patience. And, to my teachers, Joel Leach, Steve Schaeffer, and the late Louie Bellson, Ed Shaughnessy, and Nick Ciroli for their friendship, support, and inspiration.

Drumset Notation Key

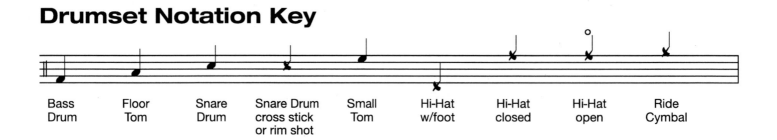

| Bass Drum | Floor Tom | Snare Drum | Snare Drum cross stick or rim shot | Small Tom | Hi-Hat w/foot | Hi-Hat closed | Hi-Hat open | Ride Cymbal |

Part 1:
Fill Concepts and Primer Practice Material

When performing big band music, the drummer is at the helm, providing the feel, groove, and pulse that make the musicians on the bandstand comfortable and inspired to play. To accomplish this, you must maintain a feeling of consistency when keeping time.

A common tendency many drummers have when playing fills is to rush (speed up) or drag (slow down) the tempo. This is often due to a coordination conflict between a player's upper and lower limbs. One example of this is when a drummer transitions from one texture or musical event (cymbal swing time) to another (drum fill on toms). To help remedy this, we recommend counting out loud to resist the urge to change tempo. Practicing with a metronome can also help you become more consistent and confident as you gain experience playing drum fills in a variety of musical styles.

Keep the Common Tone:
Rhythmic Ideas That Promote Consistency

An approach to help maintain consistency when playing fills is to keep the common rhythm and tone you're playing time on as the *foundation* for your fill. One example of this approach is to continue playing four quarter notes on the bass drum, and beats 2 and 4 on the hi-hat while filling around the kit with your hands.

Keeping your limbs sonically and rhythmically consistent as you transition from "beat to fill" can help provide the common thread that unites the beats and fills you play, promoting a more solid time feel throughout the arrangement.

Below are some alternate foot patterns to get you started. Practice these examples slowly at first, until you gain control of each foundational rhythm. The next step is to try these rhythms as the basis for your fills within the context of a musical phrase from an arrangement.

Alternate Foot Patterns in Swing, Latin, and Funk Styles

Fill Notation

Slash notation is used to indicate "time" in drum parts (Example 1) but can also be used as a substitute for written drum fills (Example 2). This alternate notation specifies improvising a fill that matches the dynamic texture and musical style of the ensuing phrase.

Slash Notation Example 1

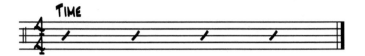

Slash Notation Example 2

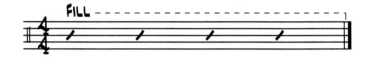

Fill Articulation

Articulate big band drummers designate sources of sound from their drum kits as they perform fills that best complement the articulation and intensity of a note or phrase.

A drum fill that leads to any articulated note or phrase is determined by:

- what section of the band is playing.

- the dynamic intensity of the phrase (loud or soft).

- the instrument's range (for example, the high or low register of the horn).

A key to dynamic fill articulation is to listen as you play your drum fills. Are your fill ideas understandable to the musicians you're accompanying? Try letting your ears point you in the right direction as you construct. Remember, your approach should always match the ensemble. Reading and understanding the articulation symbols below can help bring clarity and consistency to the longer phrases you play.

Accent (>) – Emphasize a note, and play it with a strong attack.

Staccato (•) – Play the note short and detached.

Marcato (∧) – Play the note short, and accented or stressed.

Legato (–) – Play the note smooth and connected.

Suggested Fill?

Should a drummer that is sight-reading an arrangement trust the written fill from a drum part or play something different?

This question gets brought up quite frequently. The short answer: Use your ears to determine what kind of fill works best for the music. Many composers and arrangers are not drummers, and so the written fills they write may not always be the best option. Unless it's a specific part for a movie/TV score, or the composer/arranger specifically asks that the written fill be played, the composer/arranger will most often trust that an experienced player will come up with something that's appropriate for the music.

The educational world is a little different in that many beginning jazz ensemble publications do include written bass lines, instrumental solos, and drum fills to give inexperienced players guidelines as to what to play. Once students gain more experience, however, they are encouraged to move away from the written parts and create their own solos and fills. When playing fills, the drummer should provide the rest of the ensemble with enough rhythmic information so they're comfortable with where the beat is.

Fills in Time:
Interpreting and Connecting Section Figures

In a big band, a drummer frequently reinforces background figures played by the rhythm, saxophone, trumpet, or trombone sections. Doing so adds **reinforcement** and "punch" to such figures. Section figure cues are often written above the staff on drumset parts and are normally played by just one section of the band, often behind a soloist. When supporting section figures, the ride cymbal and hi-hat rhythms normally continue uninterrupted while a background figure is played on the snare drum or bass drum.

On the following pages, you will have the opportunity to practice many different drum fills while interpreting written section figures. We suggest you practice this collection of material at a variety of tempos and dynamics. As you continue to practice these examples, our hope is that the written material will inspire you to come up with your own fill ideas. As mentioned earlier in Part 1, practice these examples with a metronome and count aloud, so the tempo remains consistent as you transition from one section figure to the next.

Play the interpreted fill examples below with the following ride-cymbal pattern, and the hi-hat on beats 2 and 4.

Ride-Cymbal Pattern with Hi-Hat on Beats 2 and 4

Fills in Time, Examples 1–30

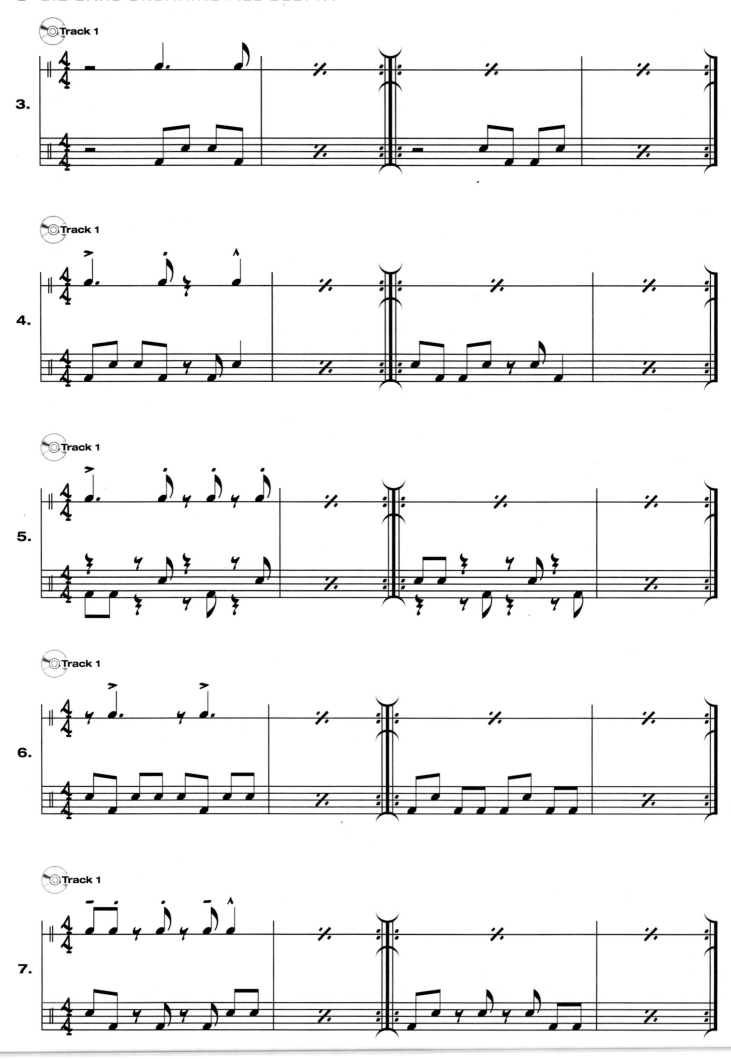

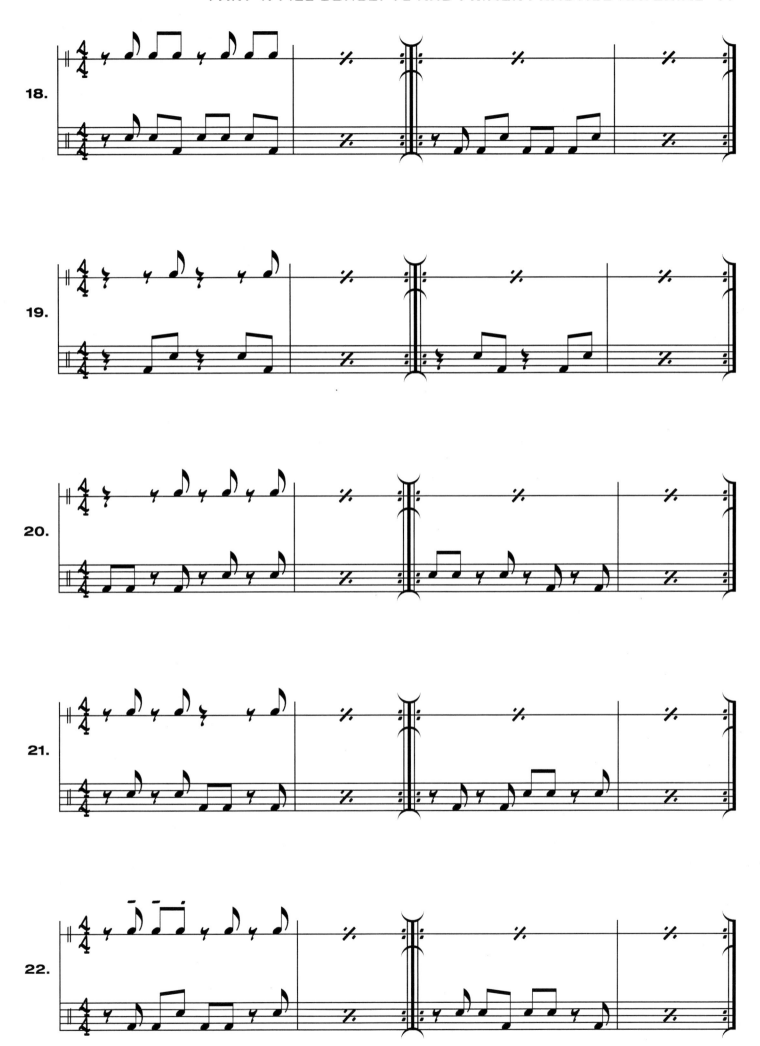

Sixteen-Measure Combination Study #1

 Track 2

Fills in Time, Examples 31–60

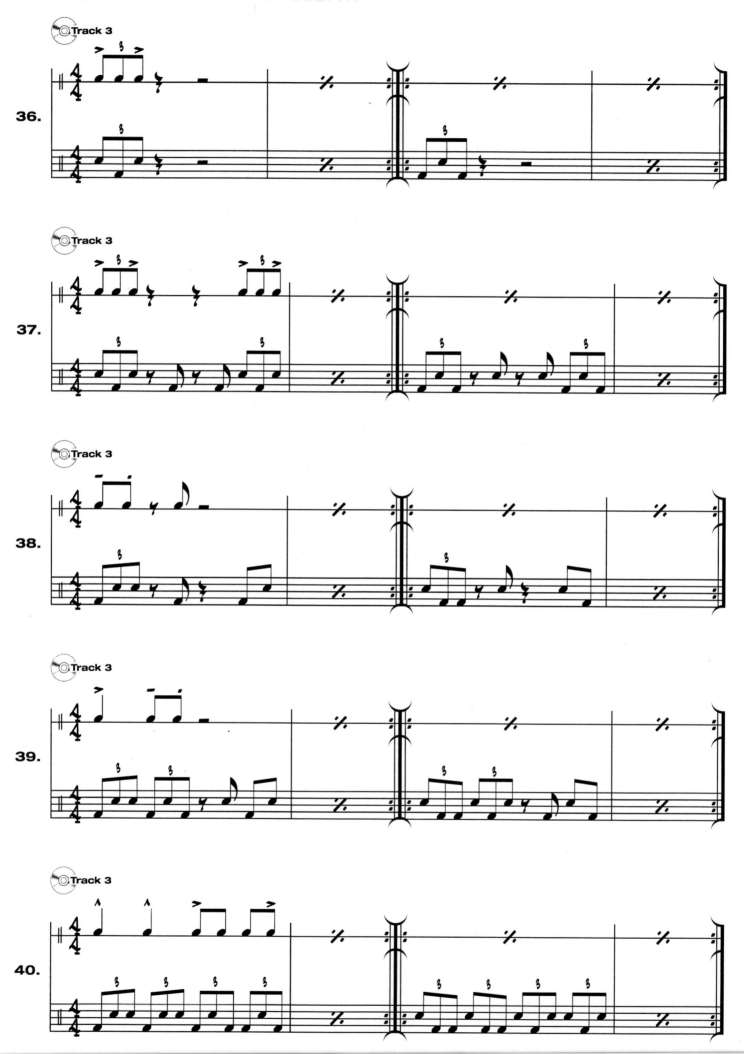

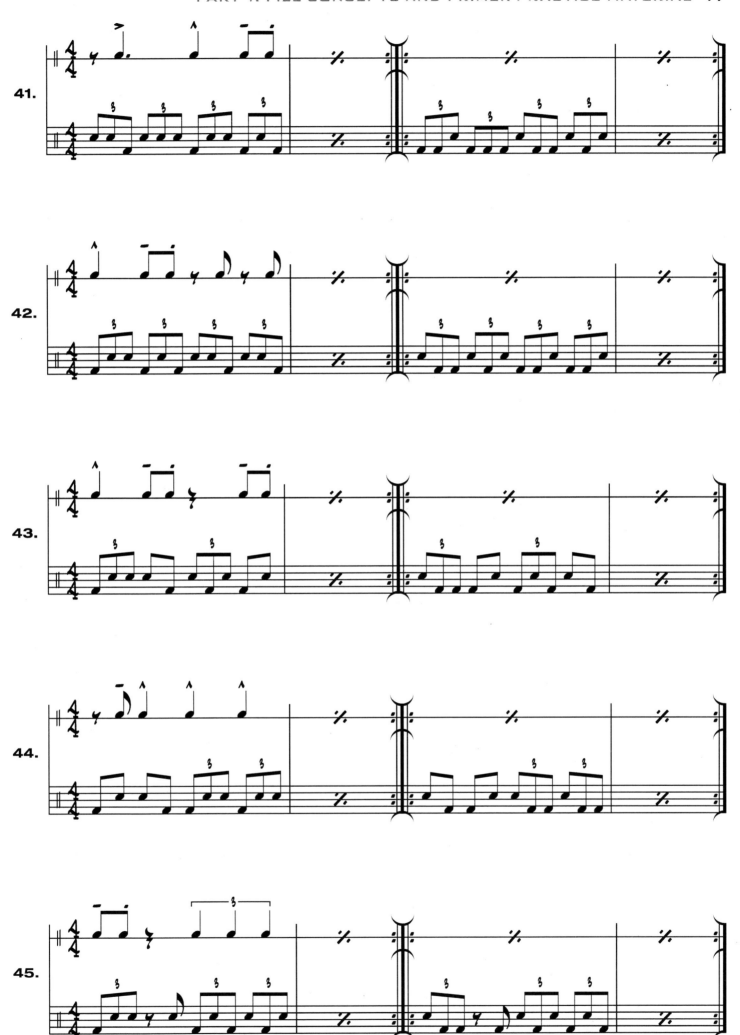

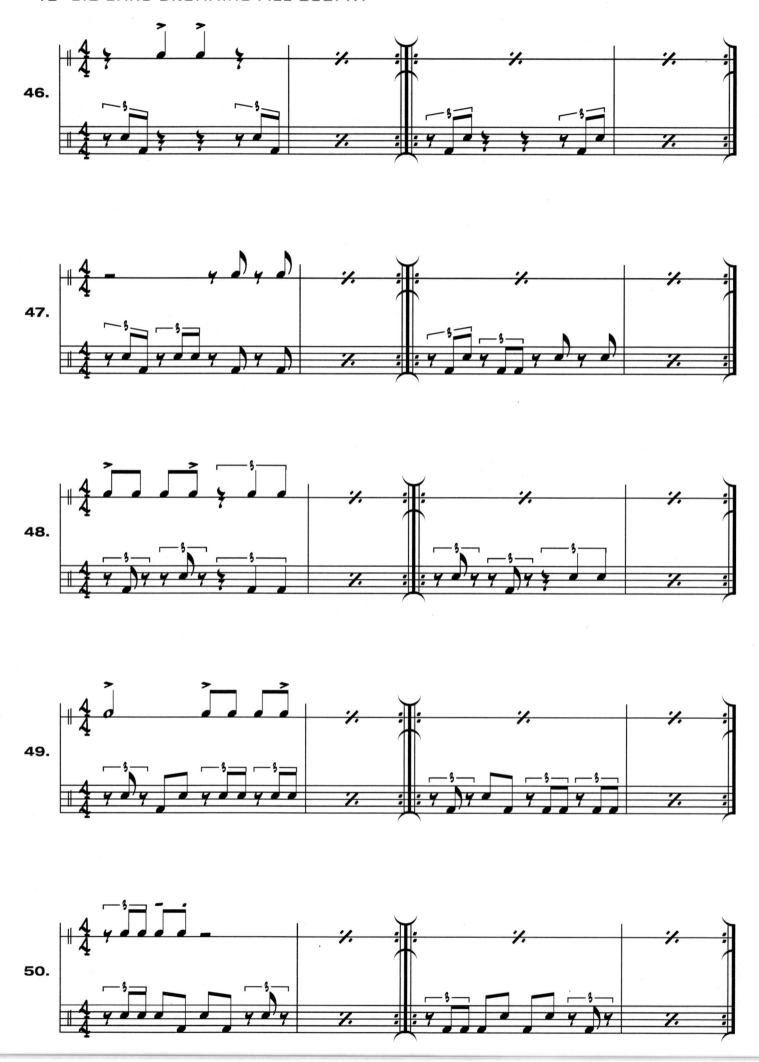

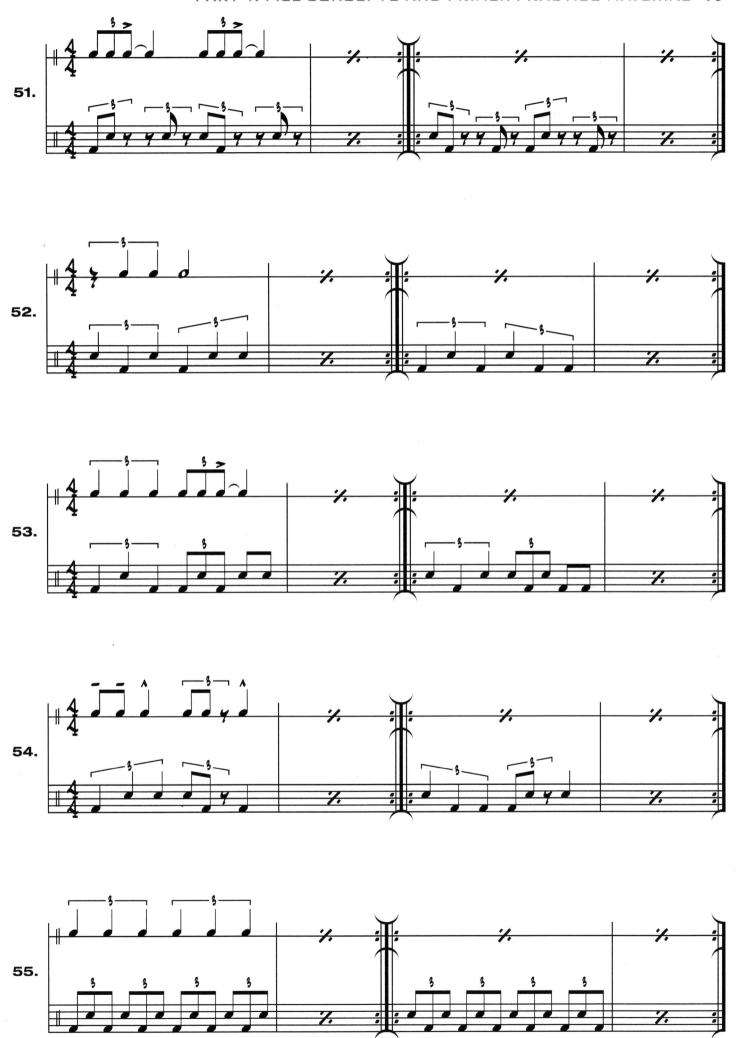

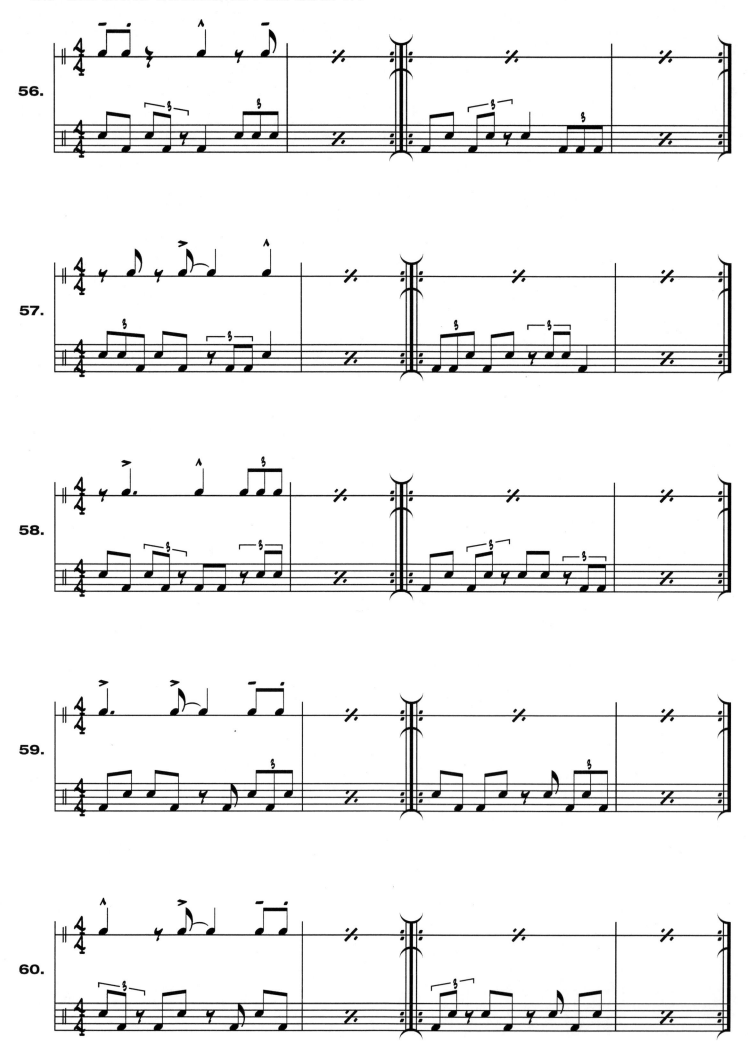

Sixteen-Measure Combination Study #2

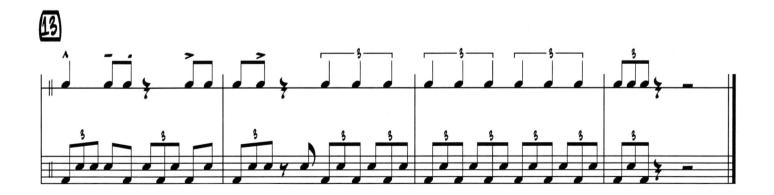

Clarity Is King!

Through our experience as big band drummers, we've learned the importance of playing fills that are clear and understandable to the band. We sometimes refer to this as the "silver platter" approach, since it provides an obvious way to hand the section or ensemble their entrance. An effective big band drum fill should match the dynamic of the resulting section, ensemble figure, or phrase. This helps guarantee that the section and/or ensemble enters with confidence.

Several factors will determine the kind of fill or set-up that should be played. When "filling" into a musical passage, a variety of contrasts should be used.

When playing section or ensemble figures, remember that the fill or set-up must remain in the style of the music. Drum fills that feel and sound good take the music from where it is to where it is going.

As you fill, listen to the ensemble and yourself to provide the keys to musical fill development. To help determine the musical context for a fill, listen to the ensemble's rhythmic information, phrasing, and dynamic approach so you can apply this information directly to the fills you compose.

Fill Development (Fill-netics)

Children learn to speak through imitating the sounds they hear from their parents. They achieve a level of competency with each vowel and consonant before they can even spell words. In terms of fill construction and articulation, we are firm believers in singing rhythmic statements using spoken words to help develop new drum fills (fill-netics). In popular usage, the words "phonics" (the area concerned with spoken sounds) and "phonetics" (the correlation between the sound and the symbol or written notation) are often used interchangeably. When applying this concept to playing fills, we are referring to the correlation between the spoken words ("Drum-ming is fun!") and the written musical notation, or phrase, that accompanies it.

Using spoken words as the vehicle for your fills can also help you gain an understanding of how a drum fill is articulated before playing it on the drums and cymbals. Of course, there are countless, creative and fun ways to come up with drum fills that can suit the music you're performing. Below are just a few spoken phrases that help illustrate this concept on the drumset.

An Ensemble Fill Set-Up:

Drum-ming   is   fun!

Don't rush or drag, the fills that you play.

Solo Fill Examples:

Don't be late, don't be late, for work, to - day.

Ac-cents give shape, to the mu - si - cal phrase.

Dynamics . . . Not All Drum Fills Are Loud!

When playing drum fills in a musical context, always listen and be aware of the relative dynamics of the music, and honor and observe them. The use of loud and soft dynamics can have a musically dramatic effect, so contrast is always a good idea. The use of accents when playing fills is also an important part of the language, as they give shape to the musical phrases. Remember, notes without accents are like words without inflection.

Targeting and Interpreting Ensemble Figures

Ensemble figures are often played with more volume to match the dynamic texture of the entire band. With ensemble figures, a drummer may choose to break away from the ride cymbal so both hands are free to fill and set up the resulting ensemble figure. For stronger ensemble entrances, a crash cymbal in combination with the snare drum or bass drum is often used. In contrast to section figures, ensemble figures are normally written inside the staff rather than above it.

A drummer is expected to set up major ensemble entrances. This concept, idiomatic to big band jazz, calls for the drummer to play a rhythm that leads to the major ensemble entrance and helps keep this entrance tight.

Ensemble Entrance Set-Up, Example 1

Ensemble Entrance Set-Up, Example 2

Instrumental Primer Target Points

On the following pages, you'll have the opportunity to practice 180 drum fills that lead to four specific rhythmic target points common to all big band arrangements (beat 1, the + of 3, 2, and the + of 4). We recommend that you practice and interpret this collection in a variety of musical styles (i.e. Latin, funk, and rock), and at a wide range of tempos and dynamics. Practice each with a metronome or with the "phrases minus drums" tracks on the accompanying CD and count aloud, so the tempo remains consistent as you transition from one example to the next. Sticking examples are not provided. We feel it's best for you, the student, to use your own stickings around the kit, in order to find what's comfortable and natural and nets the best sense of rhythmic flow and intensity.

Instrumental Target Point: Beat 1

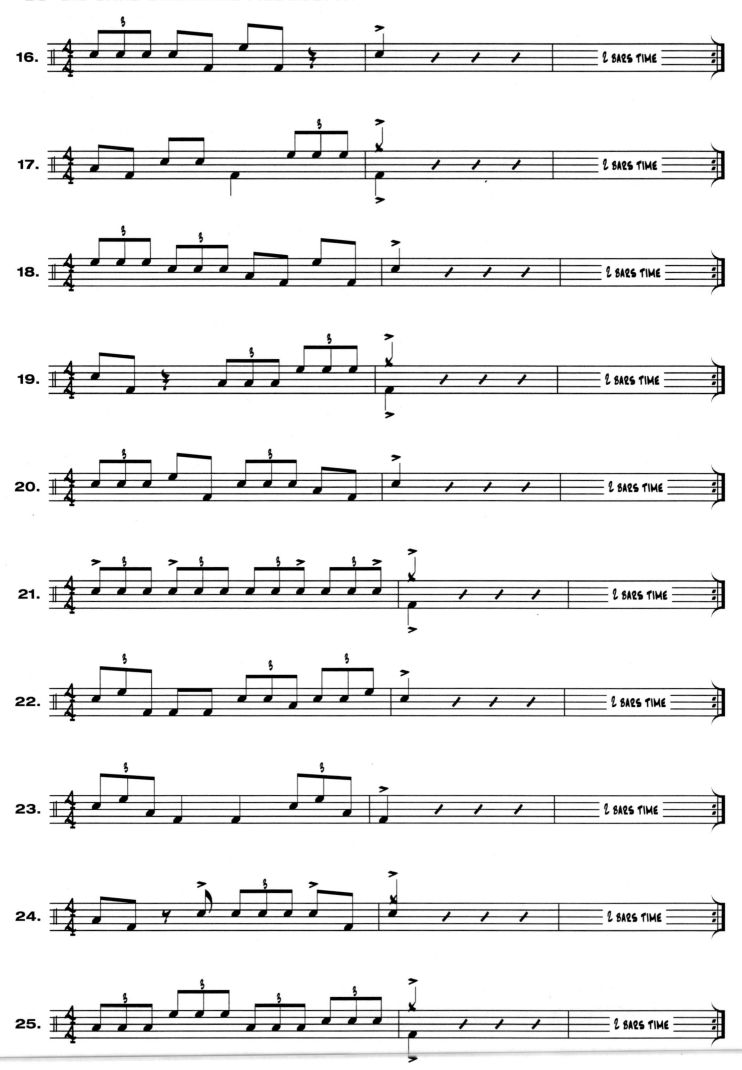

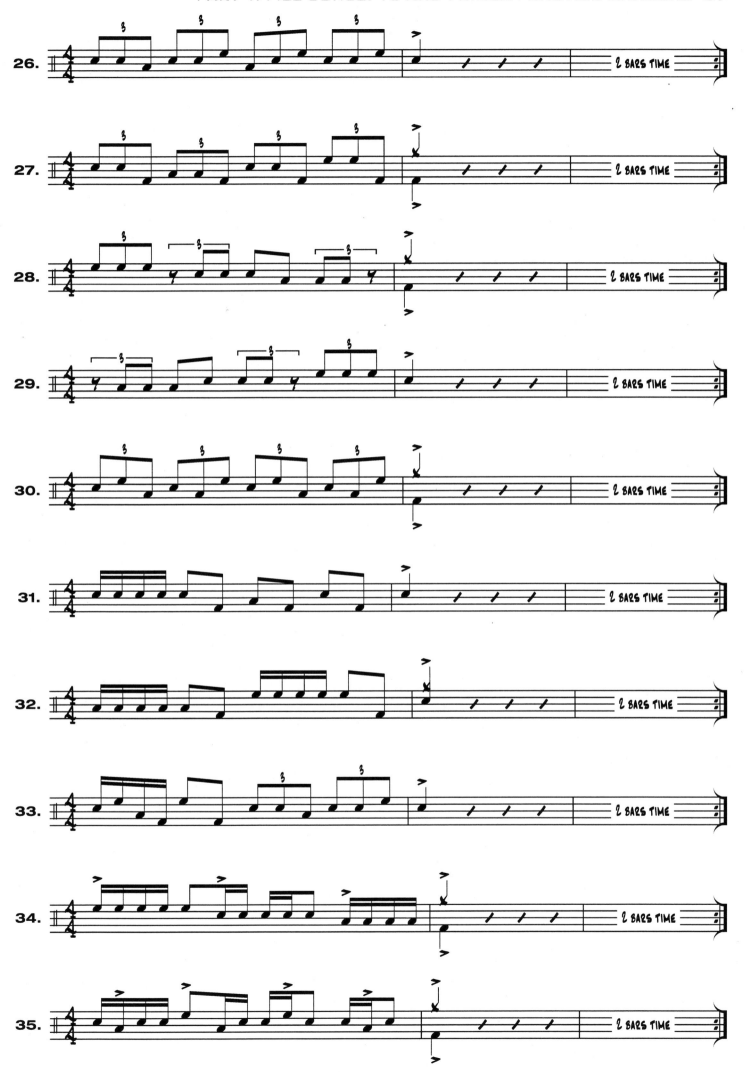

Instrumental Target Point: The + of Beat 3

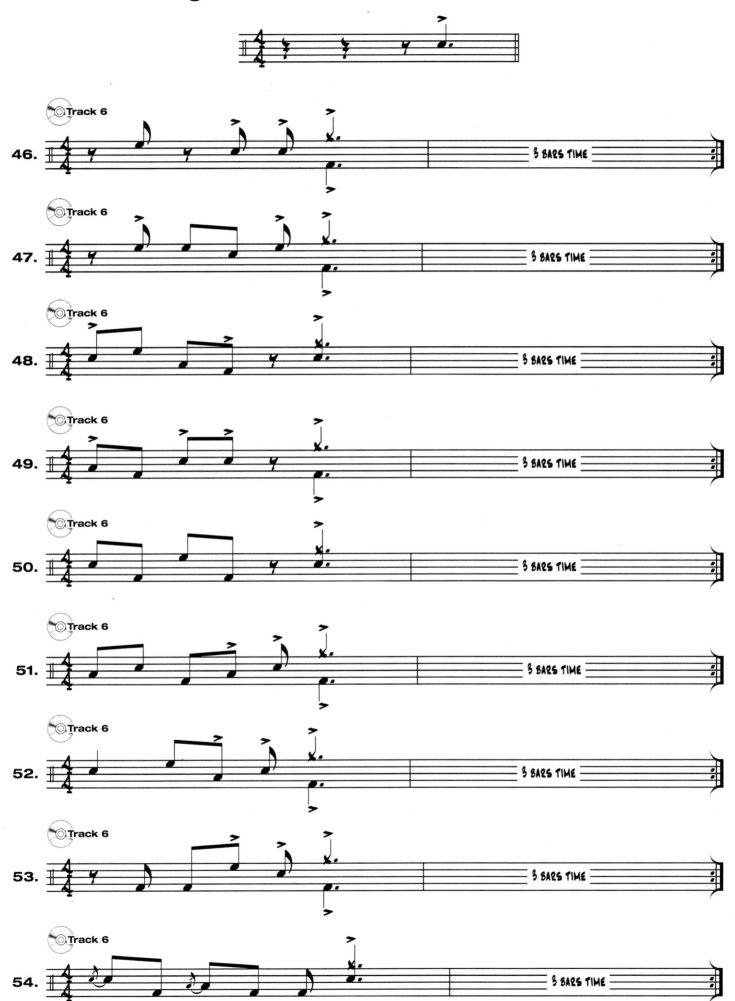

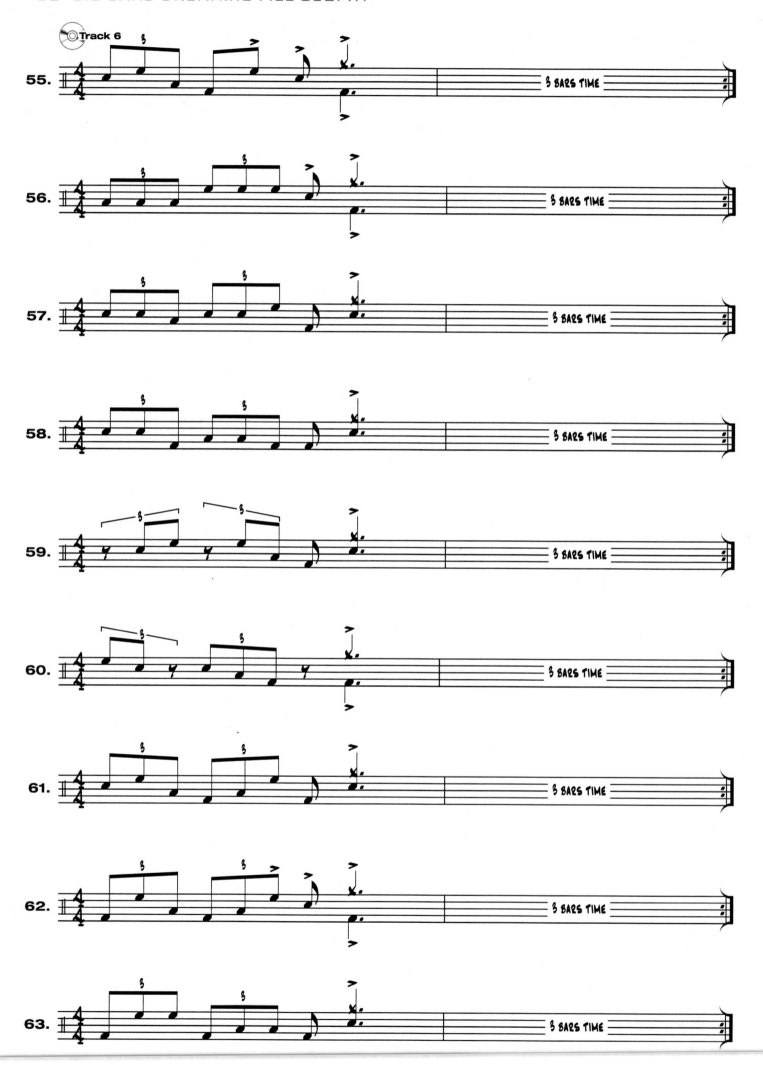

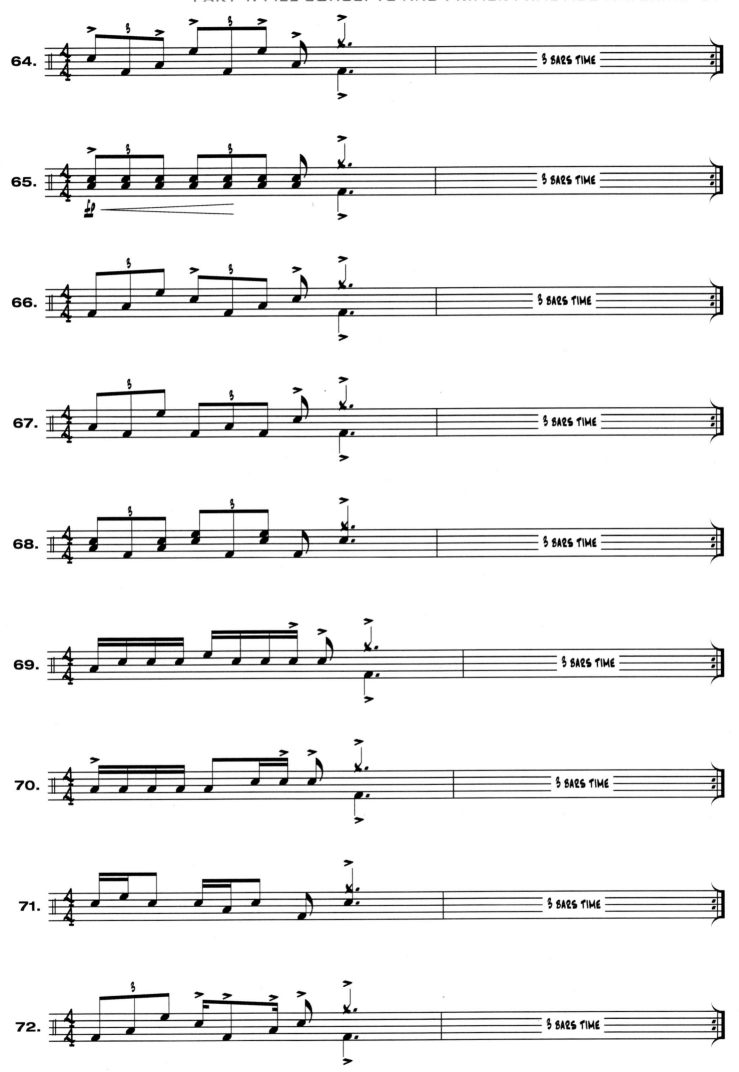

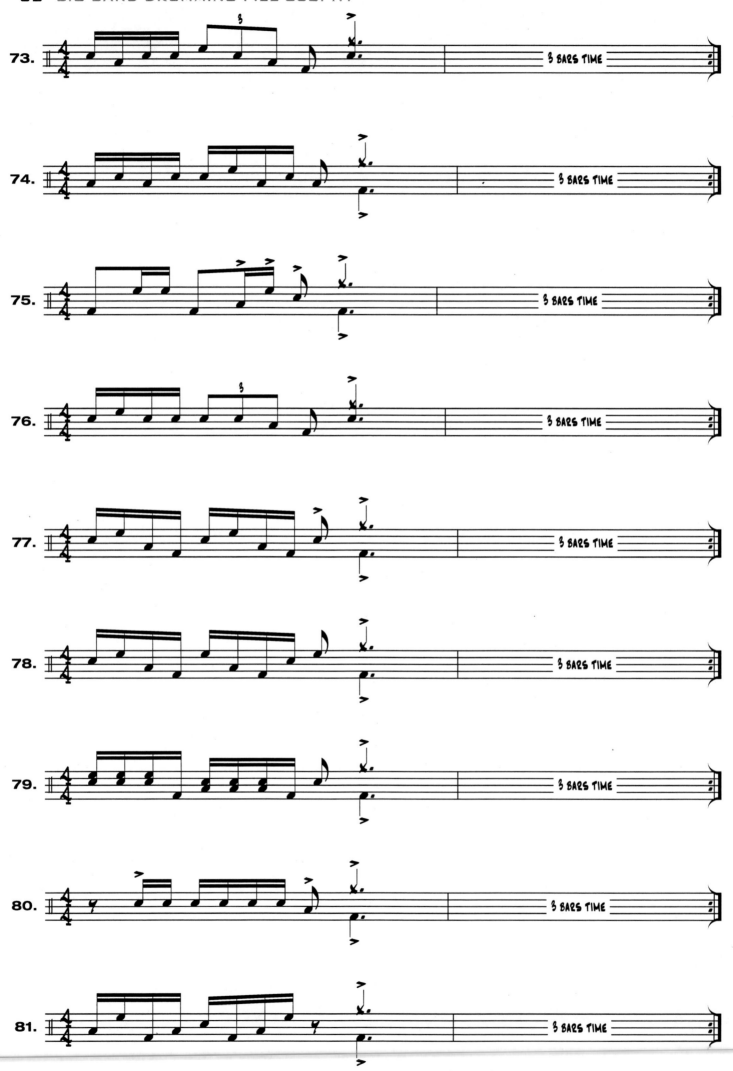

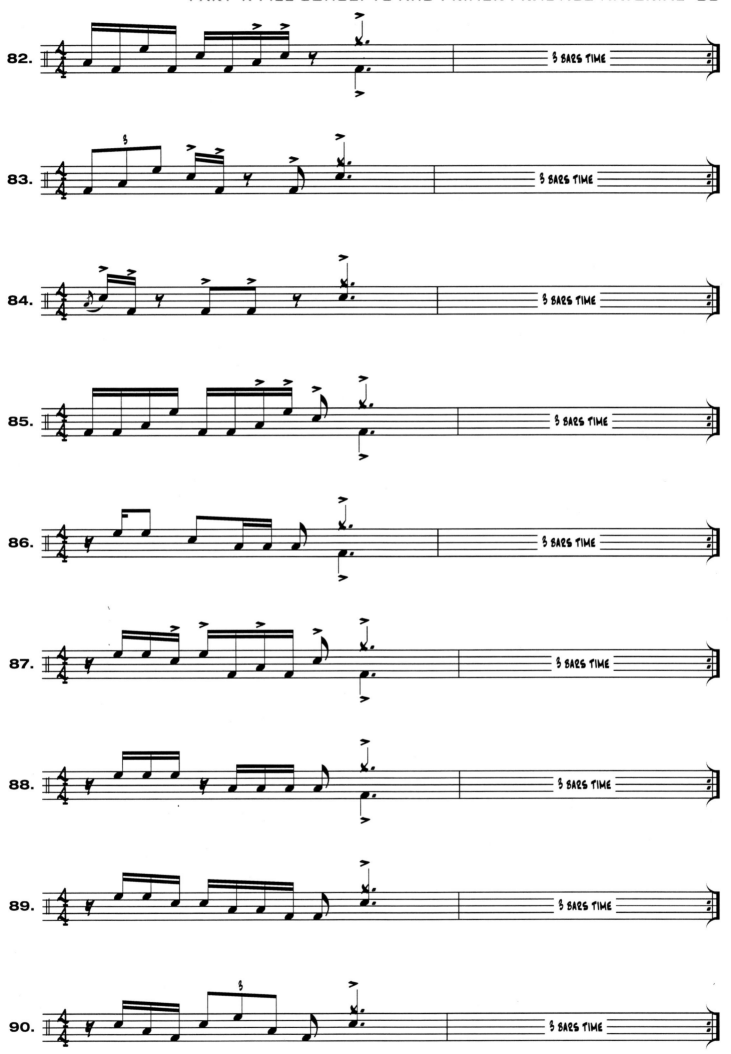

Instrumental Target Point: Beat 2

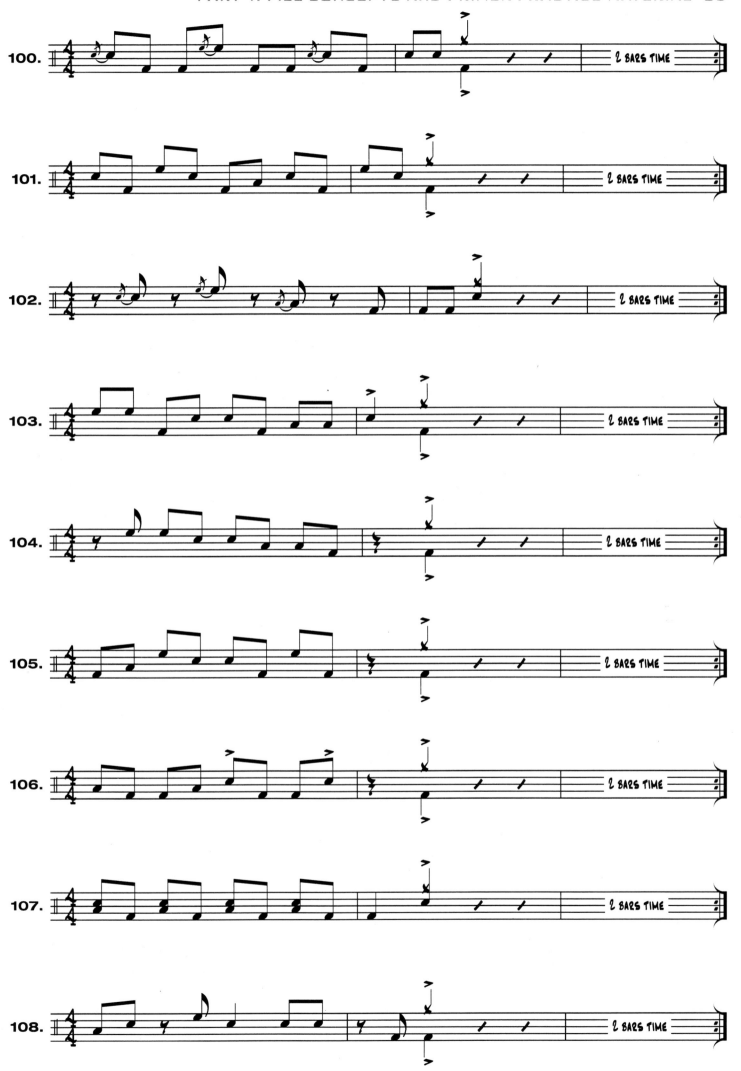

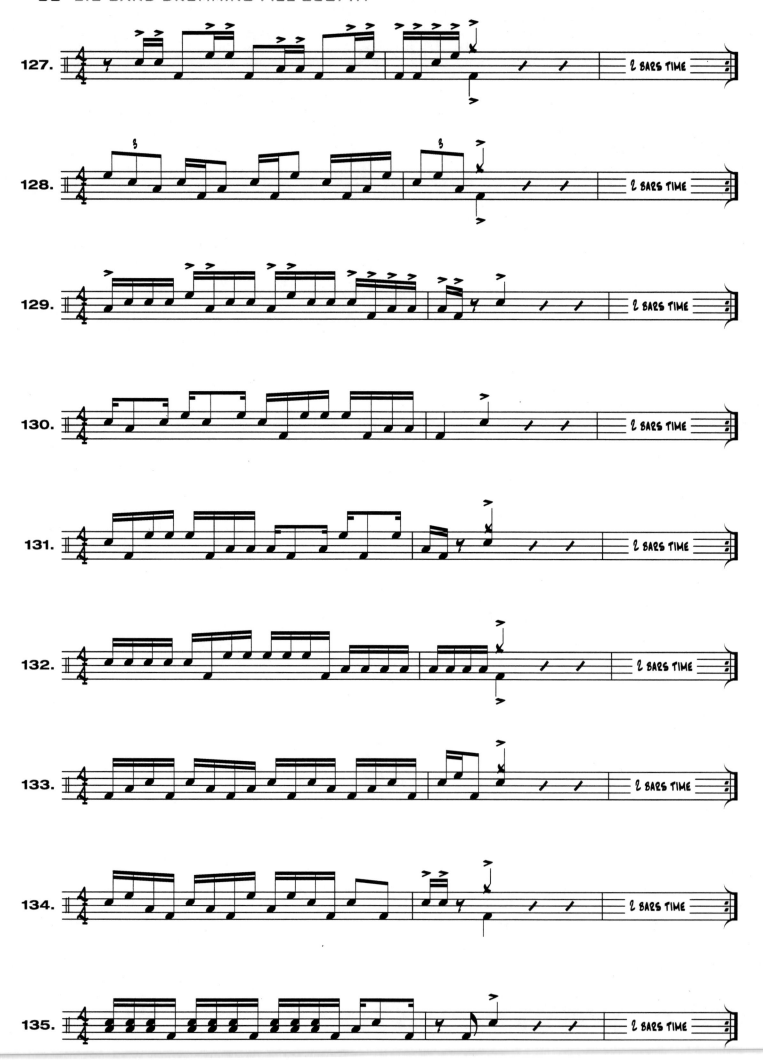

Instrumental Target Point: The + of Beat 4

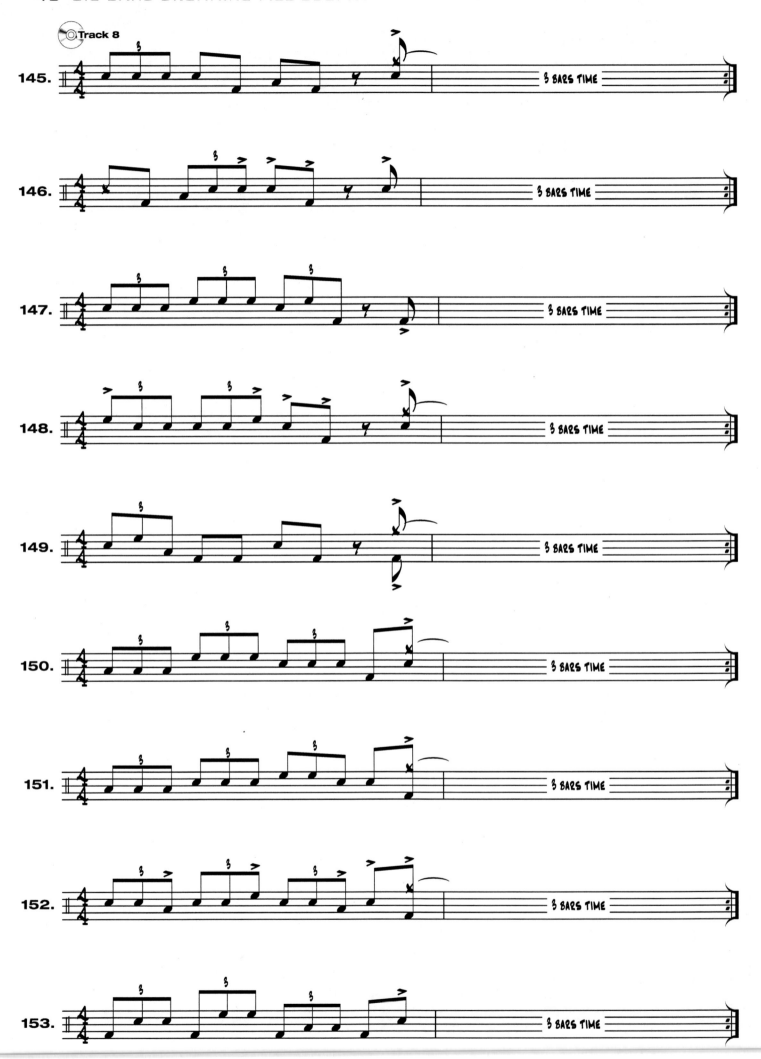

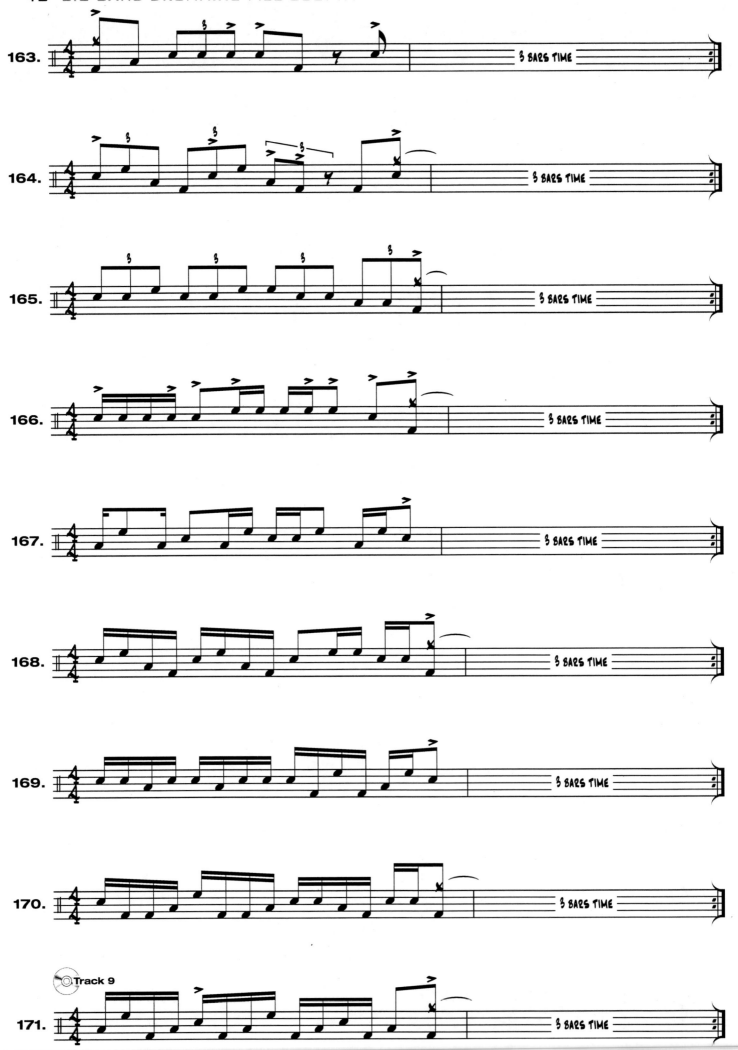

172.
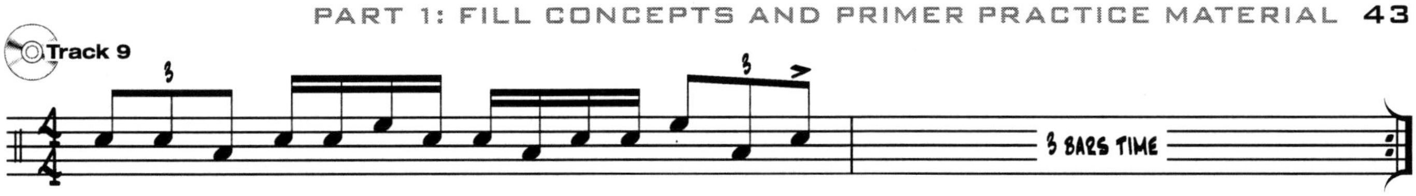

173.
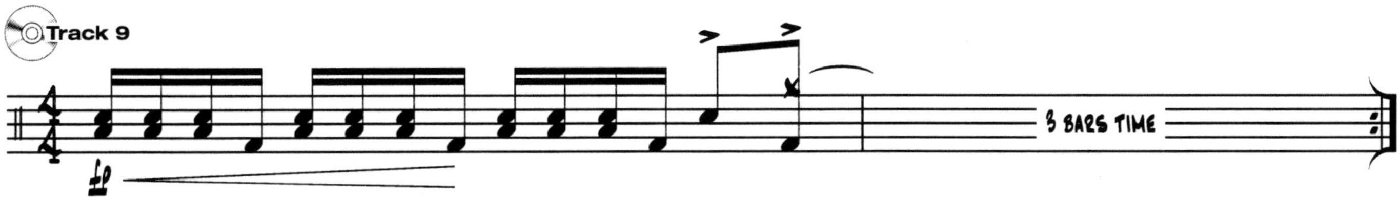

174.
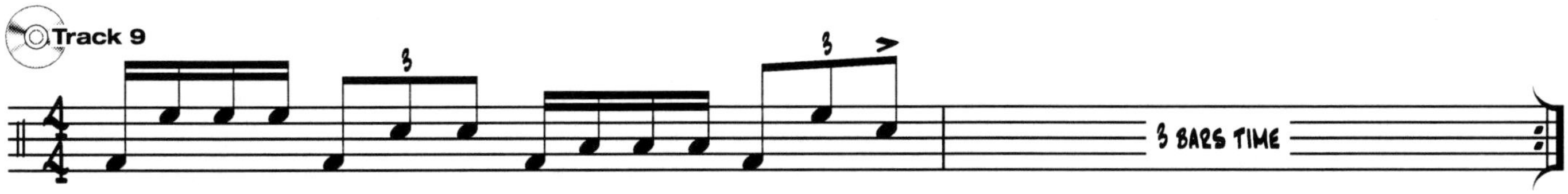

175.
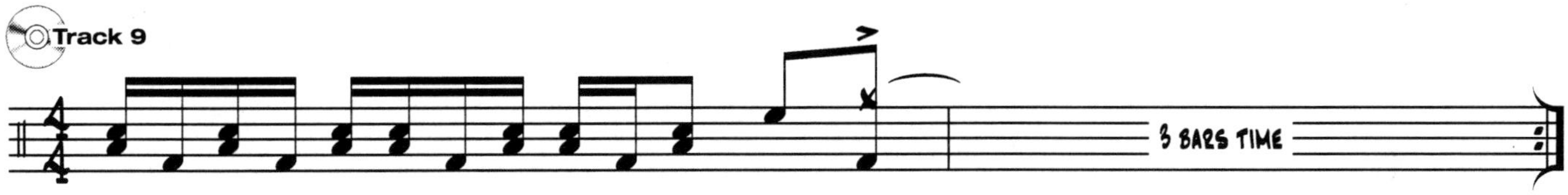

176.
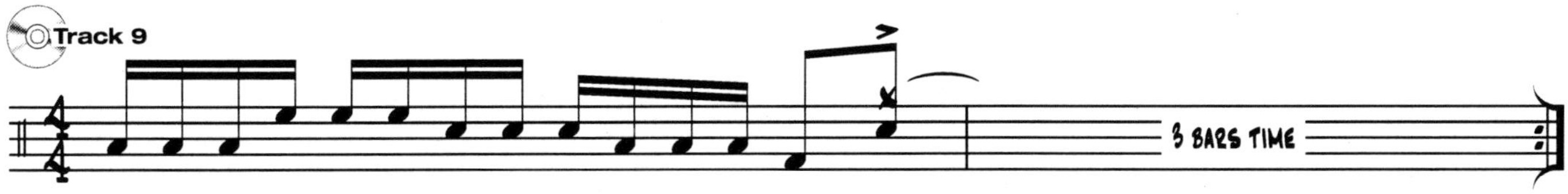

177.
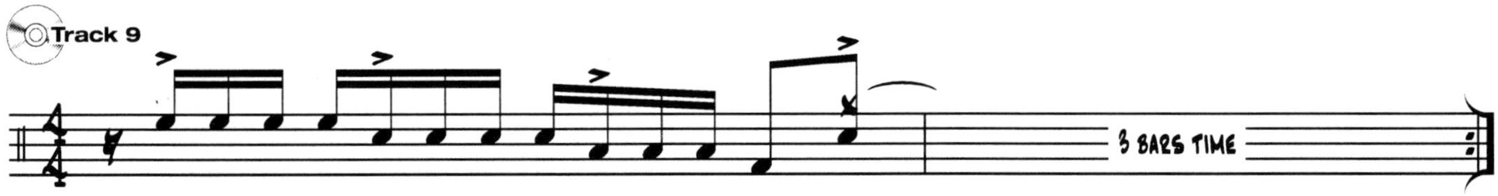

178.
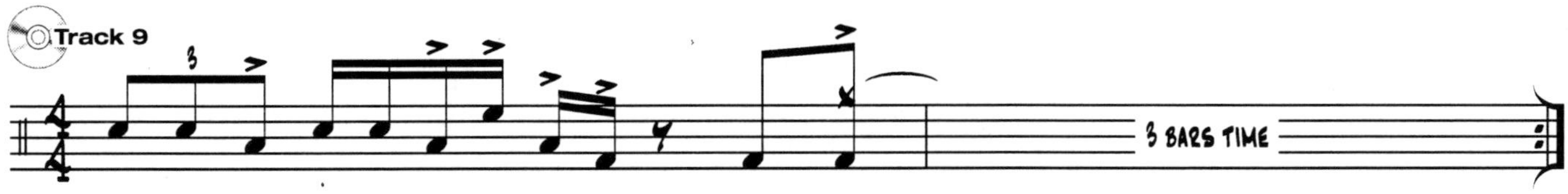

179.
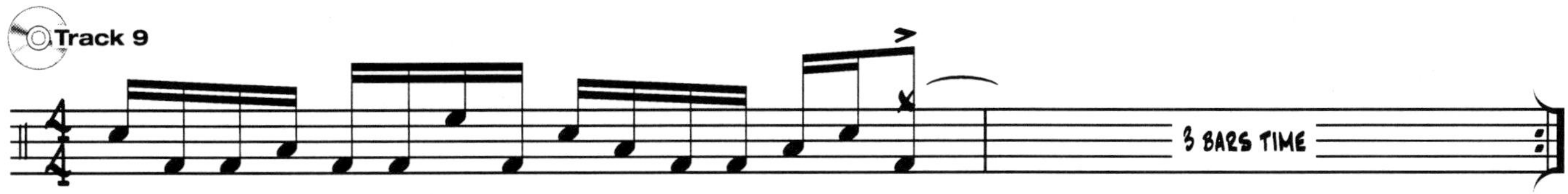

180.
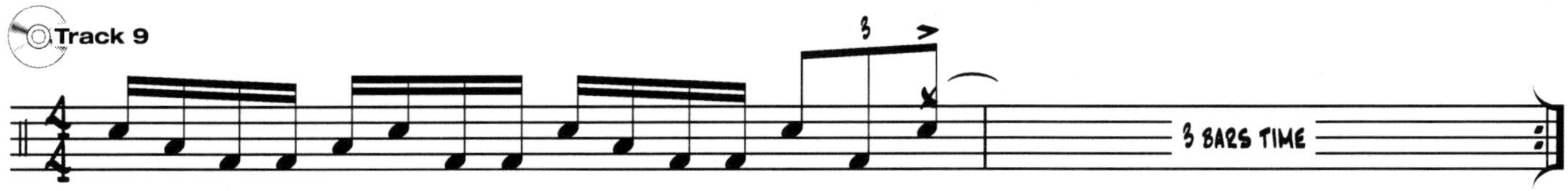

One-, Two-, and Four-Bar Phrases

The following pages contain some of the most commonly used one-, two-, and four-bar jazz ensemble section and ensemble figures. The purpose of this section is to illustrate how these rhythms might appear "on the page" in real performance situations.

The one-bar section and ensemble figures on the following pages will be presented in their two most common forms:

1. As a section figure (on the left side of the page)

2. As an ensemble figure (on the right side of the page)

With the following material, you'll have the opportunity to "improvise" your own drum fills that lead and connect each written section or ensemble figure or phrase. To get started, feel free to return to the written fill examples found earlier in the book for inspiration, or have fun coming up with your own fill improvisations. Be sure to set your metronome or practice each example with the "phrases minus drums" tracks on the accompanying MP3 CD to help maintain tempo consistency.

One-Bar Section and Ensemble Figures

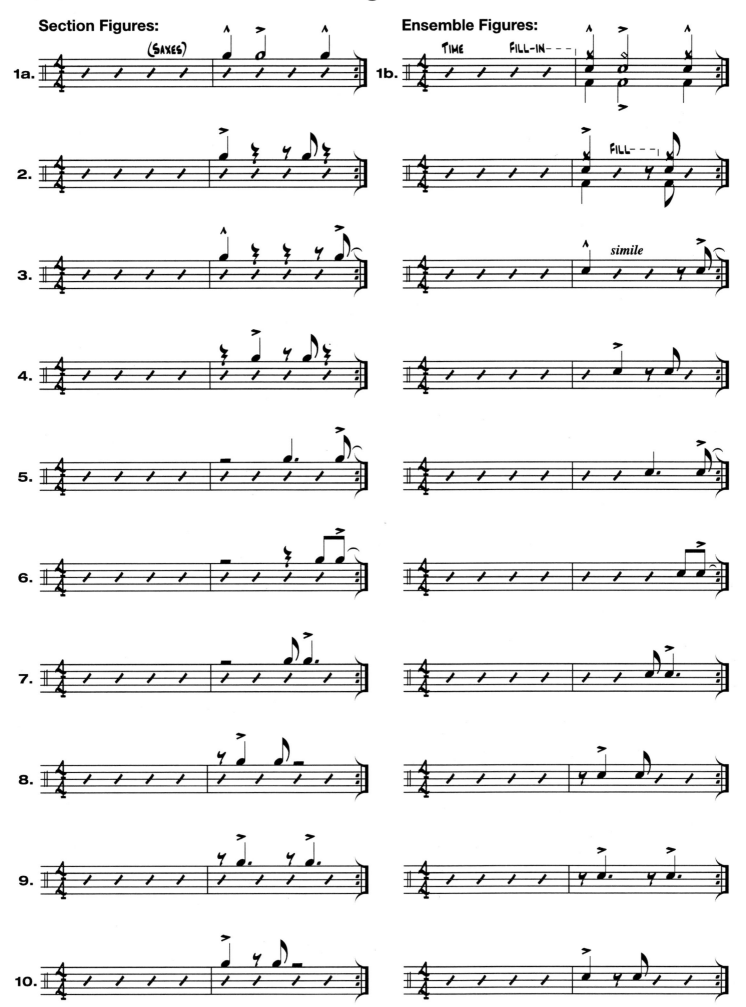

Section Figures:

Ensemble Figures:

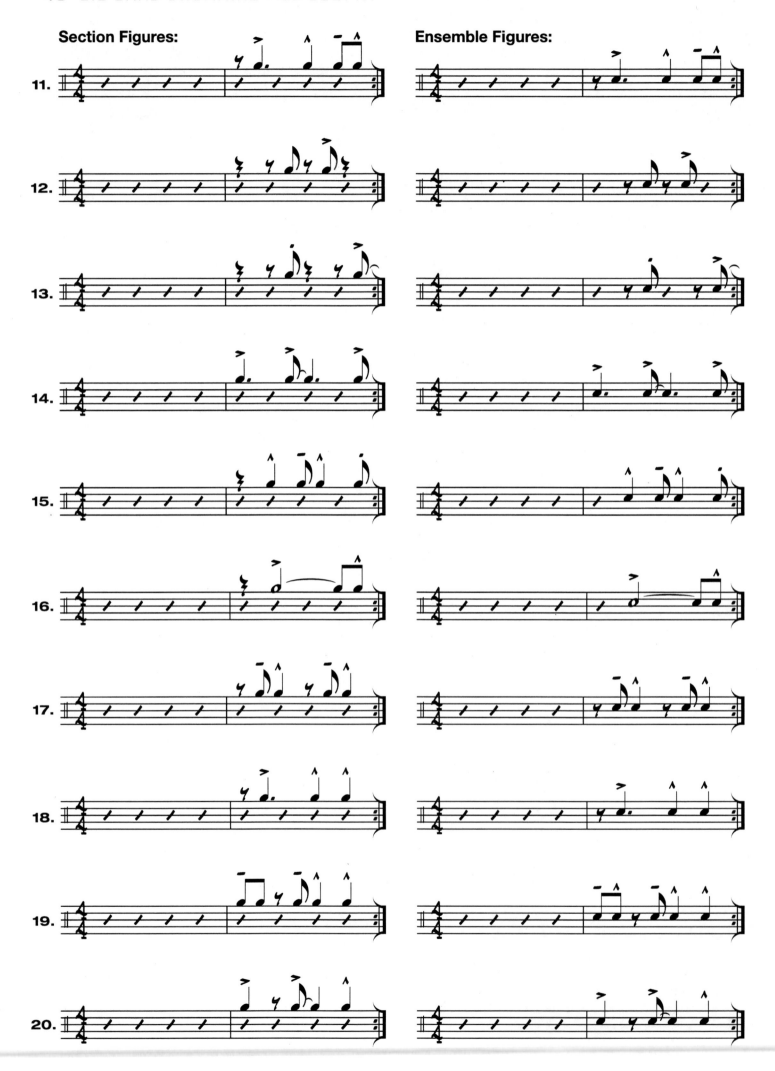

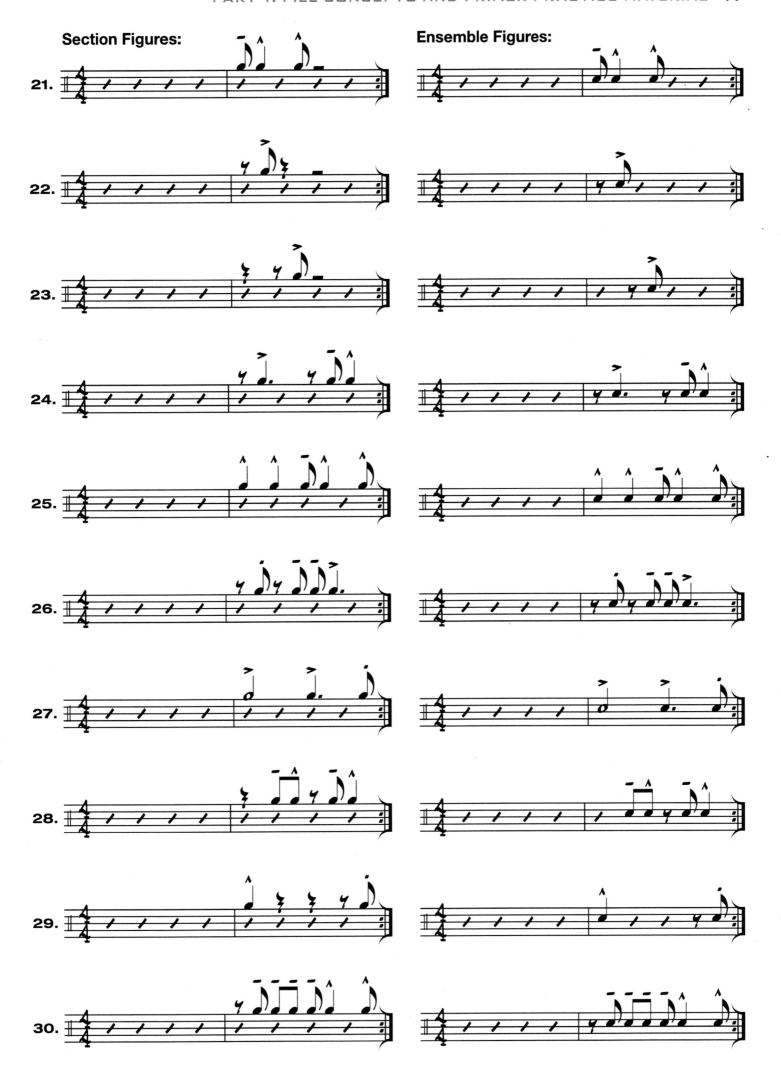

Section Figures:

Ensemble Figures:

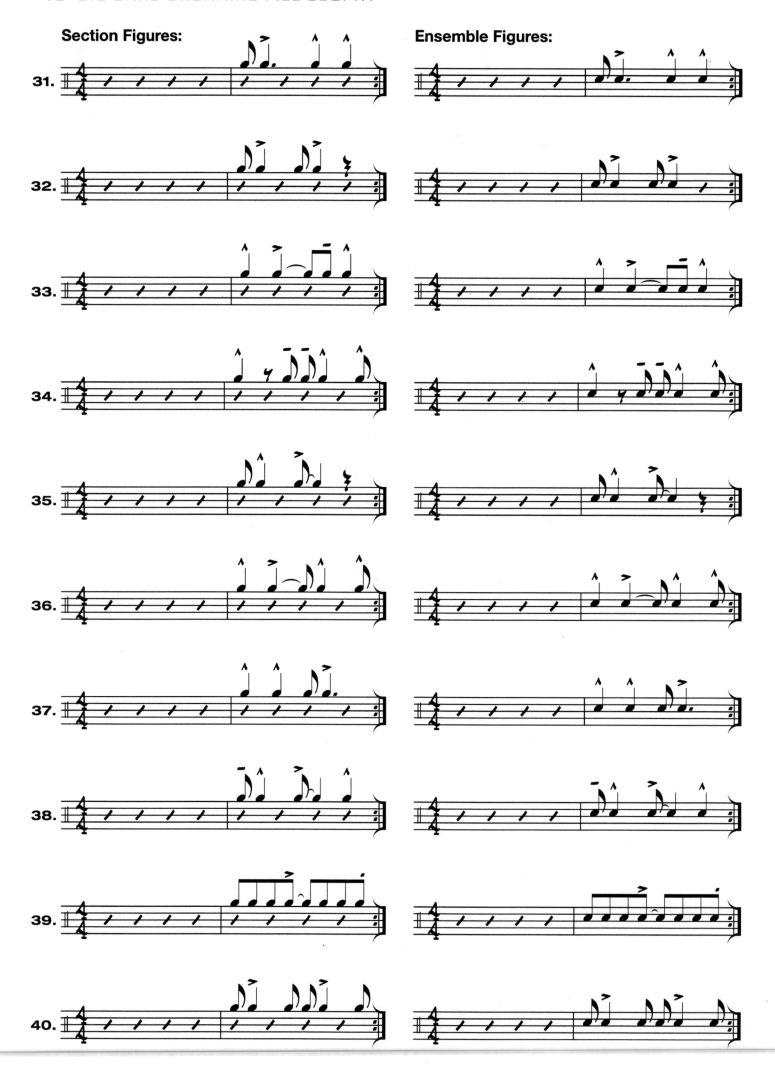

Section Figures: **Ensemble Figures:**

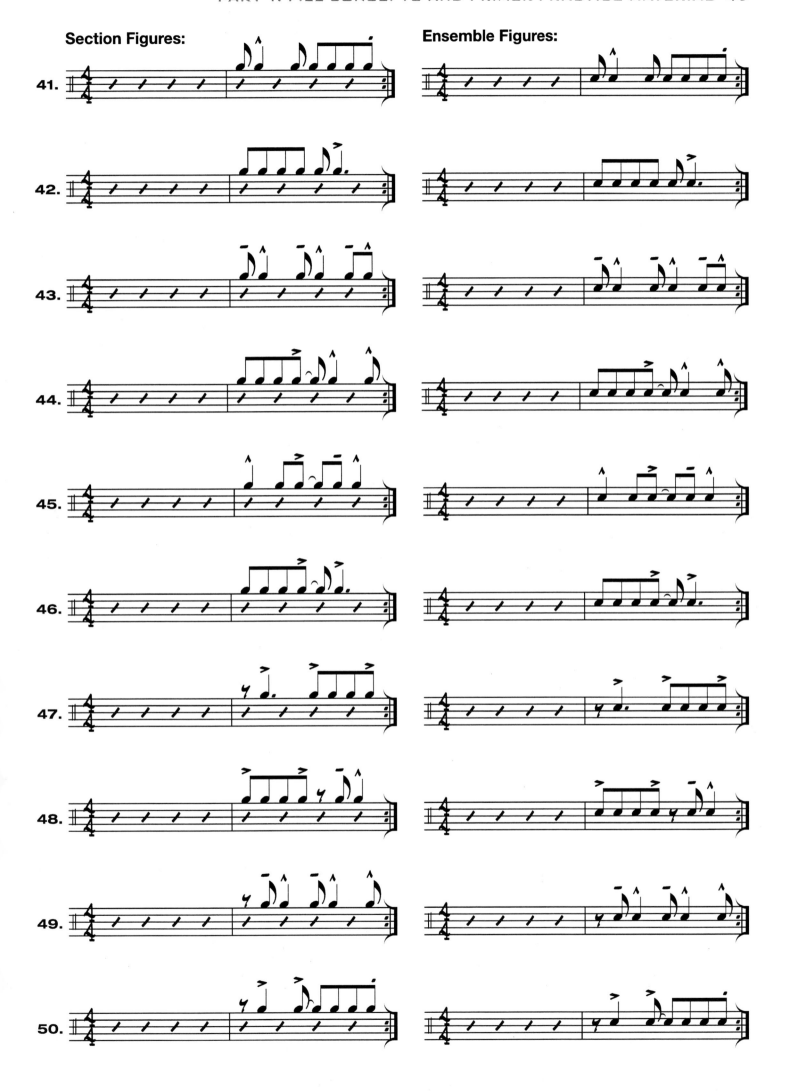

Two-Bar Ensemble Figures

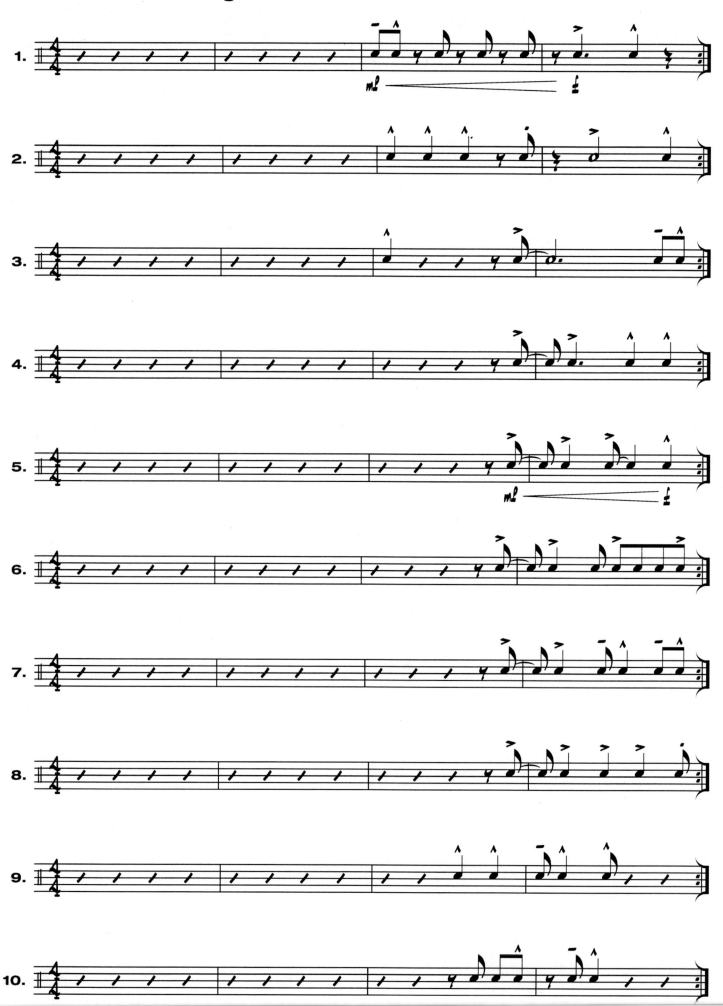

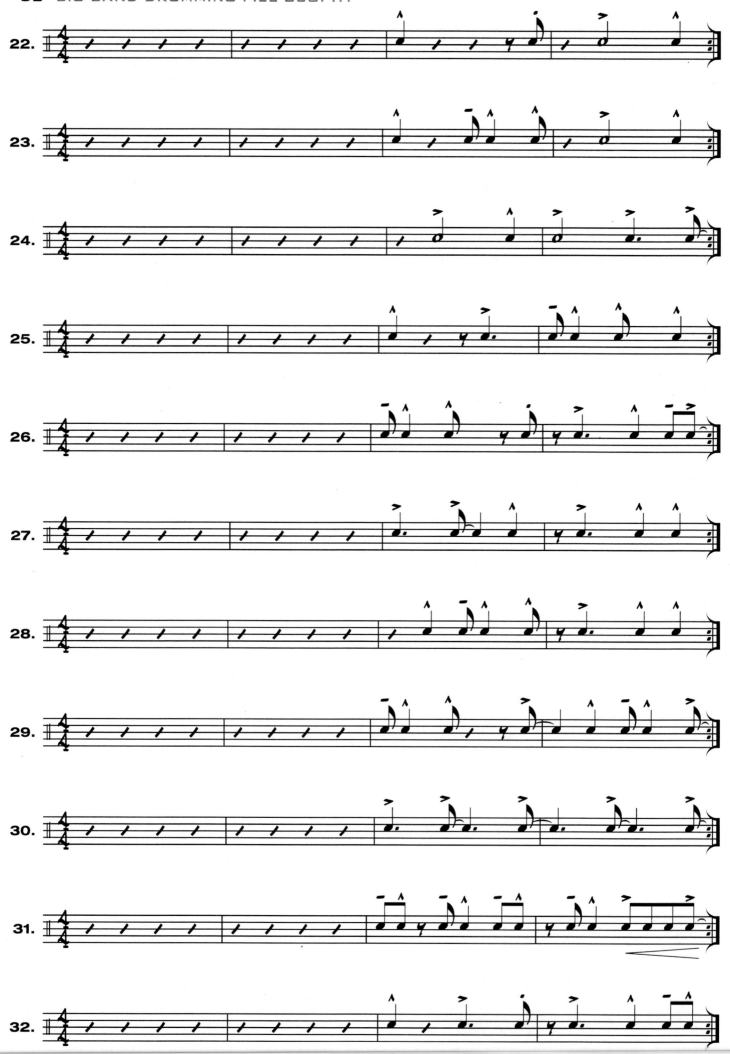

Four-Bar Ensemble Figures

Ways to Practice Fill Transcriptions

Fills can be practiced on their own in order for you to work out and perfect the required stickings and hand, arm, and foot movements. However, we feel it's best to practice fills in a context where the music and/or chart will help dictate what's best to play, as well as where and when. When practicing transcriptions, listening is crucial, because some musical styles will naturally invite a particular approach to phrasing and articulation that can occur at any point within the music.

As mentioned earlier, we suggest you practice playing fills along with a metronome or a recorded "practice loop." This will provide a steady pulse so you don't rush or slow down during the bar(s) of the fill.

The following section features three, four-measure solo examples we have slightly altered, giving you new ideas for ways to practice each. We encourage you to come up with your own applications using your own fill vocabulary, and apply each to the music you are currently performing.

Fill Transcriptions

Four-Measure Solo, Example 1   Track 10

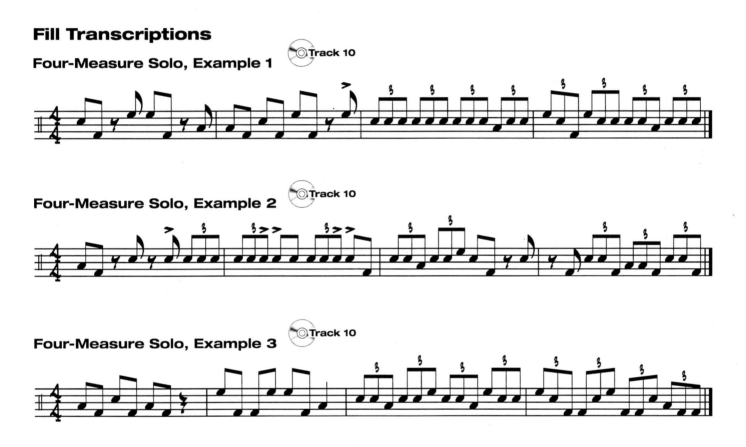

Four-Measure Solo, Example 2   Track 10

Four-Measure Solo, Example 3   Track 10

Once you have rhythmic control of the three examples above, try "re-organizing" the measures in order to transform the shape and phrasing of each solo fill. Below is the way Example 2 looks when the four-measure phrase starts on beat 1 of m. 2.

Four-Measure Solo, Example 4

Next, try combining examples. Here is Example 1, mm. 1–2, with Example 3, mm. 3–4.

Four-Measure Solo, Example 5

You can also "expand" each note value within the four-measure phrase. For example, written quarter notes would become half notes, eighth notes would become quarter notes, and eighth-note triplets would become quarter-note triplets. By expanding each note value, the four-measure phrase now becomes an eight-measure phrase. This application works extremely well when performing solos at very fast tempos.

Below is Example 3, from page 55, expanded into an eight-measure phrase.

Eight-Measure, Expanded Solo, Example 6

In addition to expanding each note value, you can also "compress" the phrase. For example, written quarter notes would become eighth notes, eighth notes would become sixteenth notes, and eighth-note triplets would become sixteenth-note triplets. By compressing each note value, the four-measure phrase now becomes a two-measure idea. This application is great for transforming jazz language and applying it in a contemporary rock or funk setting.

Below is Example 1, from page 55, compressed into a two-measure phrase.

Two-Measure, Compressed Solo, Example 7

Solo Fills

Big band drummers are frequently called upon to solo within the context of an arrangement. Such solos can be measured (for example, a four-measure solo break) or unmeasured (open solo), meaning that the solo's length is up to the drummer and/or band leader. Solo fills are intended to be exciting rhythmic statements that help draw attention to the drummer and add excitement to the music.

Below are two examples that illustrate solo fills from an arrangement. The first example leads toward the ensemble entrance, while the second fill functions as a conduit to set up the next phrase.

A Solo Fill to an Ensemble Entrance, Example 1

A Solo Fill to the Next Phrase, Example 2

Ensemble "Shout Chorus" Solos

The following full-length solos are written in the style of a typical jazz ensemble "shout chorus" passage. Practice each slowly until the ability to play them musically and at a steady tempo has been attained.

Solo #1   Track 11

Solo #2  Track 12

Fine 2nd Time

Solo #3

Solo #4

Solo #5

Solo #6

Solo #7

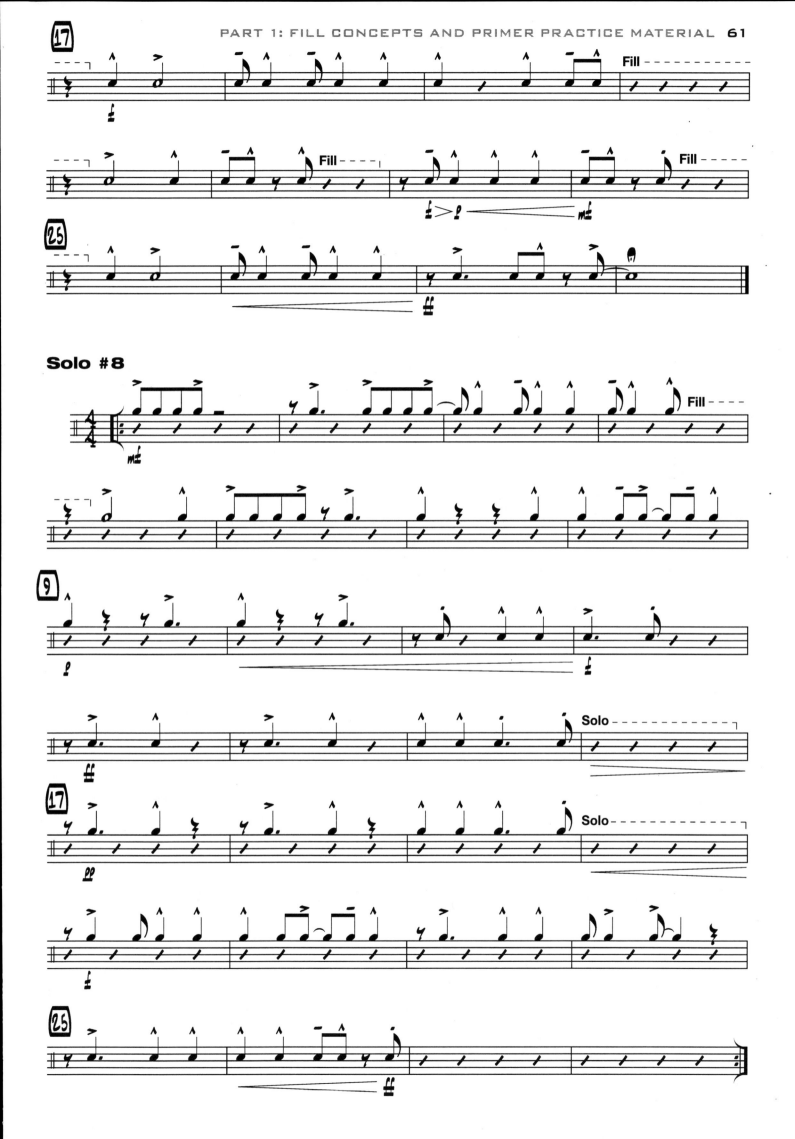

Solo #8

Solo #9

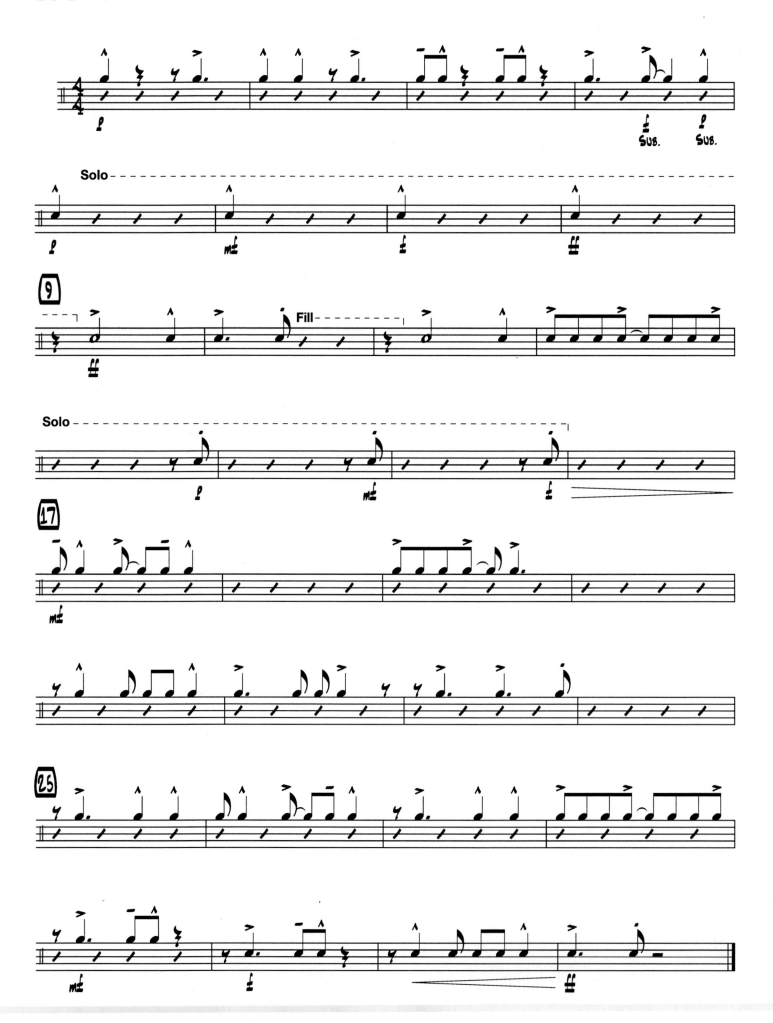

Solo #10

Play-Along Tracks

Tracks 13–26 on the MP3 CD contain "phrases (minus drums)," featuring a professional big band. We've included these tracks to help simulate a live performance situation, so you can go back and practice the written fills in Part 1.

Part 2:
Fill-in-terpretation in Context

Part 2 of *Big Band Drumming Fill-osophy* provides phrases "in context," extracted from big band arrangements. For each example, we include a short synopsis justifying the musical approach to the written phrase. As you listen and practice each example, we suggest you use the slow-down software provided on the MP3 CD. Begin each extracted phrase "under tempo," and gradually increase it until you have control of each rhythm at the desired tempo.

The following examples feature Steve Fidyk sight-reading big band phrases throughout Part 2. These chart excerpts were extracted from full big band arrangements he recorded for the newly published jazz ensemble music for Alfred/Belwin's jazz catalog. With that said, Fidyk relied heavily on the suggested fills that were written in the drum part, as well as the articulation markings that accompanied each phrase.

Intro Fill-in-terpretation

Fills featured throughout the **introduction** of big band drum parts are essential to the success of the arrangement. Since the introduction is where the tempo and subdivisions are set, the drum fills you improvise should not detract from the forward motion of the time feel. Drum fills help influence the tone, attitude, and overall dynamic, so listen carefully to the band as you choose sound sources from the drumset that best match the intensity and articulation of a phrase.

Example 1, Medium Swing Track 27

Due to the *forte* dynamic marking, I approached the initial two measures of this medium-swing introduction with a strong approach. As you listen to the repetitive loop on the MP3 CD, note the "bomb" accent played with the crash cymbal and bass drum on beat 1. This accent is of extreme importance, because it helps set up the ensemble entrance on the + of beat 1.

Example 2, Funk Track 28

Drum fills in funk charts tend to be more staccato in nature. Before the first reading of this piece, I scanned the introduction with my eyes and noticed the marcato articulations written in the first measure. I elected to accent these markings as opposed to playing the suggested fill.

This, of course, is a matter of personal preference and taste. The fill in m. 2 is important to the band because it helps bond the introduction to the initial melody phrase.

Example 3, Latin Track 29

Following the two-measure rest, I set up the ensemble figure on beat 2 of m. 3 by playing a crash cymbal and bass drum accent on beat 1. This is another example of a "bomb" accent, now played in a Latin-style arrangement. To help complement the marcato articulations in m. 3, I interpreted these rhythms on the hi-hat using sticks. The fill in m. 4 acts as a conduit that bridges the initial ensemble entrance and connects it to the piano's montuno pattern featured in the next phrase. Again, I elected to improvise my own fill as opposed to what was suggested on the part.

Example 4, Medium Swing Track 30

This example illustrates the power of a measure of eighth-note triplets as they lead the ensemble into the introduction of this swing arrangement. I took liberty with the suggested written fill in the pickup measure, and "doubled it" on the snare drum and floor tom. In addition to the written crescendo, I also accented beat 1 of this fill so the band could clearly feel where it was. Doing so helped ensure that the band entered precisely in m. 1 of the arrangement.

Example 5, Swing Shuffle Track 31

The swing shuffle is a very special rhythm built upon the first and third eighth notes of a triplet grouping. This repetitive rhythm needs to be present in order for this style to be clearly defined as a shuffle. For the initial phrase marked "cross stick" on the snare drum, I read the part as written without any fills, and the overall effect was crisp and clean. The rhythm written on the + of beat 3 in m. 2 (crash cymbal and bass drum) helps to complement the long articulation played by the ensemble.

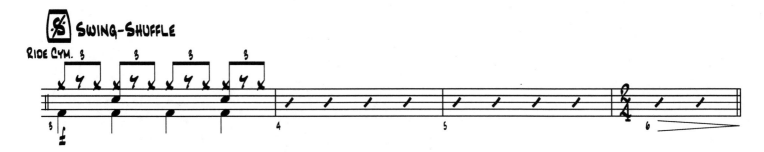

Example 6, Funk Track 32

The arranger uses "rhythmic notation" throughout the introduction for each written ensemble figure to help achieve a desired effect from the drummer that is crisp, punchy, and in unison with the horns. I apply these rhythms as a "measured outline" by filling around them without detracting from the precision of each low-brass entrance.

Example 7, Medium Swing Track 33

The written rhythm featured in this introduction excerpt is written on the bass drum space without articulation markings. Before I sight-read this, I made an educated guess based on my experience as to how the lower instruments in the band would articulate it. Since this is a background rhythm played by a section of the ensemble, I kept the swing pulse firm and steady on the ride cymbal and hi-hat, and played minimal fills throughout the phrase.

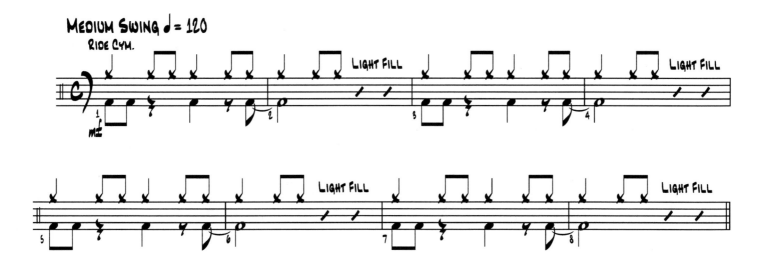

Example 8, Bright Swing Track 34

For this up-tempo introduction, I lead the ensemble into their entrance on beat 2 of m. 1 with a fill that resolves on the downbeat. The staccato articulations in this phrase are essential because of the measures of "rest" that help frame each motif. I filled throughout the introduction and concentrated on these markings in order to help minimize the amount of cymbal "ring-over" into the measures of rest.

Example 9, Medium Swing Track 35

This is a classic example illustrating fills that help set up and connect ensemble figures throughout an introduction. In order for the band's entrance to be strong, it's important that your fill "lead in" (or set-up) matches the dynamic of the ensuing band figure (in this case, *fortissimo*). Take note of the interpretation in the final two measures due to the written decrescendo that helps lead the arrangement to the first statement of the melody.

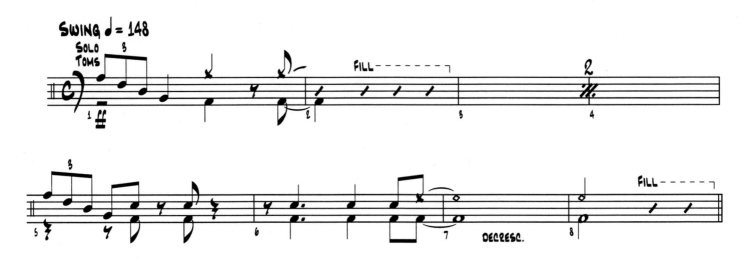

Example 10, Be-Bop Track 36

Be-bop is a specific style of jazz that first originated in New York in the early 1940s. Its characteristics include complex harmonies and rhythms, and very fast tempos. This example begins with phrasing that is typical in be-bop style arrangements (rhythm in 3/4 time superimposed over a 4/4 time signature), as the phrase bounces between the trumpet and saxophone sections. To provide a solid foundation, I begin the arrangement with a solid quarter-note accent on the bass drum to help establish beat 1. The phrase continues featuring the sound of the hi-hat cymbals and the many ways of integrating them into the fabric of the phrasing.

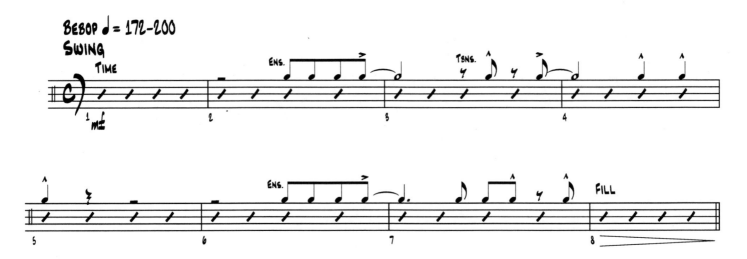

Example 11, Latin Track 37

This phrase begins with a montuno rhythm played by the pianist. For this arrangement, a montuno can best be described as a repetitive syncopated vamp that helps establish the time feel and phrasing for the composition. Since there is no indication (or "cue") on the drumset part illustrating this rhythm, I simply listened closely as I counted my rests and applied this vamp as a "rhythmic outline" for the drum fills I played.

Example 12, Medium Up-Tempo Swing Track 38

The introduction for this example begins strong and gradually decrescendos. It's important to note that the number of measures in this phrase is "odd" or nonsymmetrical, and the fills I play help bring stability to the phrase. The part indicates to play the eighth notes short, starting in m. 3. However, I interpreted the + of beat 4 in this measure (and in m. 5) using a "long" interpretation, based on the written phrasing in the pickup measure. To acknowledge the decrescendo that begins in m. 8, I transition from the ride cymbal to the hi-hat cymbals and continue to fill and connect each written rhythm.

Outro Fill-in-terpretation

Fills written throughout the **outro** of big band drum parts help bring an arrangement to a close. In many instances, outro drum fills carry the music from the final melody statement to the coda section of an arrangement. This often requires the drummer to "look ahead" and jump from the bottom of the first page to the "lower right" of the last, in order to catch this transition. These arranged sections are commonly bridged together with a drum fill, and it's important to understand the significance of providing rhythms that are clear and understandable for your band mates. Doing so can help avoid the possibility of a musical "train wreck," where the entire ensemble fails to enter a phrase with confidence. As intro fills bring the arrangement "in," outro fills help take the arrangement "out," so listen carefully to the band to help decide what type of fill works best for the concept of the phrase you're interpreting.

Example 13, Half-Time Funk Track 39

The two-measure solo fill from this example helps bring the arrangement to a strong close. As you'll hear on the MP3 track, I combine the eighth-note phrasing from the half-time groove into my fill, providing continuity and intensity so the music continues moving forward into the final ensemble phrase.

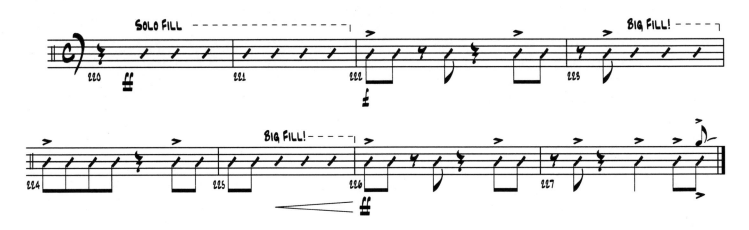

Example 14, Medium Swing Track 40

With each staggered entrance, beginning with the rhythm section at m. 71, the phrase crescendos. Throughout the phrase, I maintain the pulse throughout on the ride cymbal and hi-hat while filling and connecting each written figure using simple swung eighth notes and eighth-note triplets.

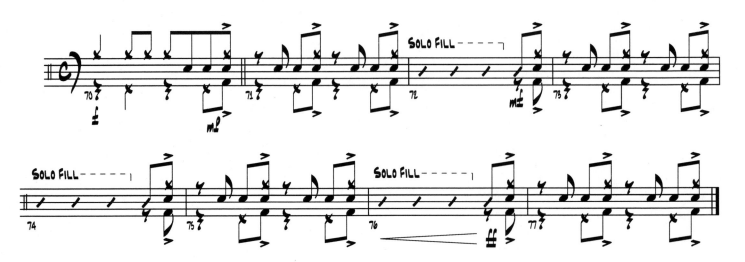

Example 15, Bright Swing Track 41

This phrase leads to a fermata in m. 111. Although there weren't dynamics written, I elected to play each fill within this phrase at a strong (*forte*) dynamic level. Often times when a fermata appears in the final measure of an arrangement, an opportunity arises for the drummer to play a short, extended solo. As I improvised, I watched the conductor and released with the band's cut-off, playing accents on both the crash cymbal and bass drum. Doing so allowed the cymbals to ring and the overtones to dissipate gradually. To hear more examples of this solo approach, check out recordings of Buddy Rich, Sonny Payne, Louie Bellson, and Harold Jones from the *Fill-in-spiration Selected Discography* at the back of the book.

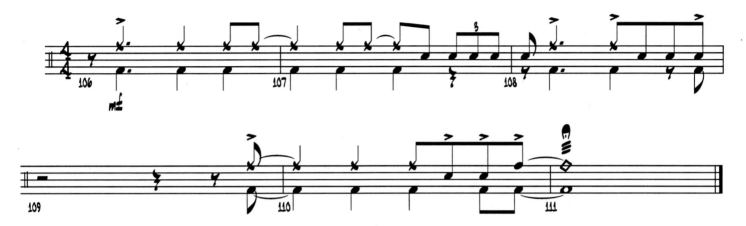

Example 16, March-Like Groove Track 42

The final six measures of this piece are written at a *fortissimo* dynamic level. Because I was sight-reading, I played mm. 95–96 of the example as written, but interpreted each quarter-note triplet grouping on the floor tom with the bass drum and crash cymbal to help match the low brass and bass texture. Even though it's not written, at m. 97 I play "four on the floor" with the bass drum to help keep each subdivision accurate as they cascade from section to section. The sixteenth-note fills on the snare drum work well to set up the final bar played in unison.

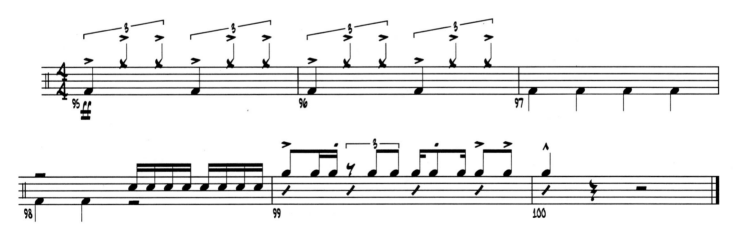

Example 17, Medium Swing Track 43

As you first listen to and practice the outro below, play with confidence and articulate each ensemble rhythm to help bring this medium-swing arrangement to an exciting close.

Example 18, Latin Track 44

Because this montuno phrase is voiced throughout the band (beginning at m. 103), I chose to play this rhythm on the cowbell, snare drum, and bass drum (even though it wasn't written that way on the drum part). I came to this determination as I played the arrangement from front to back, and noticed this reoccurring theme, which inspired me to come up with different rhythmic combinations to add variety to the piece. The fill I played in m. 108 is not written on the drum part, but I felt it was necessary to help ensure a strong ensemble entrance in m. 109.

Example 19, Medium Up-Tempo Swing Track 45

This example features the sound of wire brushes. The phrase begins with a gradual decrescendo, and then builds dynamically in mm. 163–164. I keep the texture consistent with the brushes and treat the majority of the written figures as low brass backgrounds voiced on the bass drum. For the figures in m. 164, I fill on the snare drum and voice the ensemble rhythms on the bass drum and sizzle cymbal. Take note of the marcato articulation on the + of beat 4 in m. 164. It's important to interpret this rhythm "short" so that your sound doesn't ring through into the following "rest" measure. I help set up the final band figure, which occurs on the + of beat 1 in m. 166, with a soft accent on the bass drum and sizzle cymbal. This helps to ensure that the band enters softly and with precision.

Example 20, Funk Track 46

This example begins with a three-measure time lead-in as a vehicle to set up the *fortissimo* ensemble figures that help bring this arrangement to a close. I keep the groove strong and steady as the "framework" to bring in the band for the final four measures of the coda. I also play a strong "bomb" accent on the crash cymbal and bass drum in m. 78 to cue the beginning of the coda section.

Fill-in-terpretation in Support of the Melody

Example 21, Medium Swing Track 47

As you listen to the MP3 track, I treat most of the written figures (embedded into the beat on the drumset part) as saxophone and brass background figures. Because these figures are punctuating portions of the melody, I keep the pulse solid and set up these figures with minimal fills. This allows the melody to be clearly heard and the time to keep flowing.

Example 22, Latin Track 48

This simple example illustrates how a drum fill can mark the end of a melodic phrase. Measure 33 caps the end of the second (A) section of the melody and, to acknowledge this, I play a tom fill (integrated into the beat) that resolves to a crash cymbal on beat 4. This wasn't written, but I internalized this important part of the form because it leads the phrase into the bridge section.

Example 23, Latin Track 49

This example caps the end of the shout chorus section with a one-measure drum fill that helps set up the restatement of the melody. As I sight-read this phrase, I paid particular attention to the articulation markings for each ensemble rhythm in m. 83. I "doubled" this rhythm on the snare drum and floor tom, giving this figure substantial punch.

Example 24, Medium Up-Tempo Swing Track 50

To help support the melody and the written figures with brushes (for continuity), I play fills and connect each rhythm on the snare drum. I integrate the marcato articulation in the first ending as a springboard to start my fill, which continues throughout m. 21.

Example 25, Funk Track 51

To help support the melody, I stress the rhythm section figures (written in the bass drum space) with the bass drum or splash cymbal. As you listen to the MP3 track, notice that I didn't play any fills. I used this approach to help keep the time crisp and centered so the melody can be clearly heard. Although it's not indicated this way on the part, at m. 3, I decided to add a snare drum "backbeat" on beats 2 and 4. Of course, this is a matter of personal preference, as the way the part is currently written works fine. The beauty of big band drumming is that we're "in the driver's seat" musically, and have the opportunity to make choices and interpret the music as we see fit.

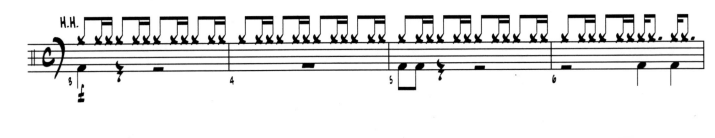

Example 26, Funk Track 52

This example illustrates fills that set up ensemble figures, as well as major sections of the form. For example, in the bridge section of this melody, I play time on the ride cymbal cup and catch the bass figures on the bass drum. To help mark this new section of the form, I play an accent on the crash cymbal and bass drum. Notice that the fill in m. 30 helps transition the phrase to the guitar solo section beginning at m. 31.

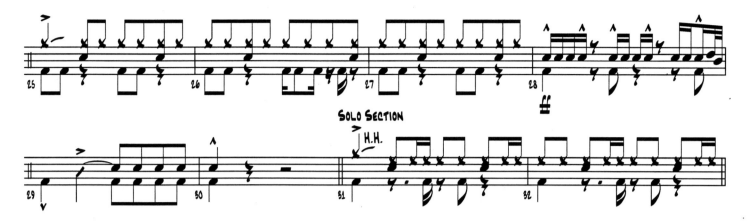

Phrases That Frame the Solo Section

Example 27, Medium Swing Track 53

The example below illustrates a phrase that crescendos from *mezzo piano* to *fortissimo* and builds excitement and musical tension. The fill at the end of the phrase sets up the ensemble figures in m. 47 and ultimately leads to the solo section. On the MP3 track, notice the accent played on the bass drum and crash cymbal on beat 1 in m. 47. This "bomb" accent assures that the band will enter squarely on beat 2 with the written marcato quarter note.

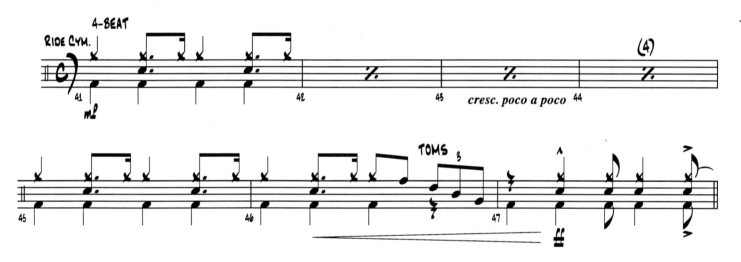

Example 28, Bright Swing Track 54

The following example demonstrates a solo fill, written in m. 33, that leads to a phrase with ensemble figures (*fortissimo*). This phrase acts as a conduit to a tenor solo. As I sight-read this phrase, I pay particular attention to the articulation markings, as well as the ensemble figures embedded in the lower portion of the staff.

Example 29, Medium Swing Track 55

This eight-measure example acts as a transitional phrase, moving the music from the melody section of the tune to the subsequent ensemble soli. During this transition, I connect each accented rhythm with clarity and intent.

Example 30, Be-Bop Track 56

This phrase leads to the tenor solo, and gradually gets louder with each staggered reed and brass entrance. I keep the pulse strong as I play set-up fills, articulating each section and ensemble entrance. In m. 75, notice that I interpret the marcato quarter notes on beats 1 and 3 as "short," with a stick shot, and "answer" this rhythm on beats 2 and 4 with the bass drum. This is one simple example of rhythmic counterpoint. To hear more examples of this approach "in action," check out recordings of Mel Lewis and Nick Ceroli from the *Fill-in-spiration Selected Discography* at the back of the book.

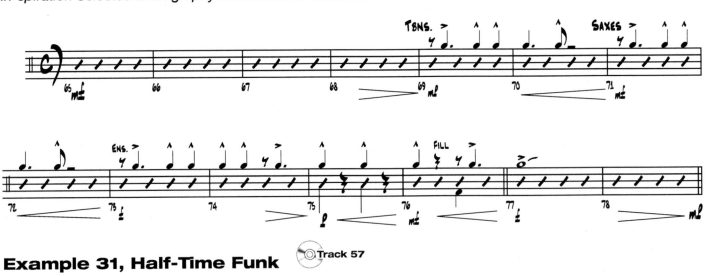

Example 31, Half-Time Funk  Track 57

This example illustrates two-measure ensemble trades with the tenor soloist. Throughout this phrase, I provide the foundation for the ensemble and soloist by keeping the pulse strong and the subdivisions consistent and integrating the figures into my time feel. This is a very common approach to accented ensemble figures in a funk context. The key to playing this style is to avoid breaking the groove.

Example 32, Medium Swing Track 58

The following phrase features the last eight measures of the melody, which crescendos to an ensemble figure. The fill is extremely important because it helps connect both phrases and set up the ensemble eighth notes on the downbeat of m. 47. The fill into the tenor solo helps make the transition smooth.

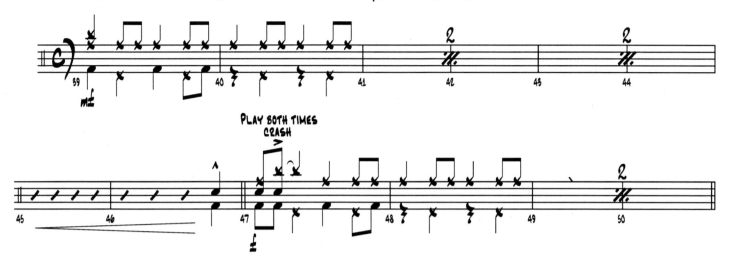

Example 33, March-Like Groove Track 59

For this example, I take the rhythms played by the rhythm section, reeds, and brass, and voice them on the cowbell, snare drum, and bass drum. I then embellish them slightly by adding fills and accents "in-between" each written rhythm. Starting in m. 38, these figures are written as "cues" on top of the staff. At the end of the phrase, I interpret the quarter-note triplet groupings between the floor tom and crash cymbal/bass drum.

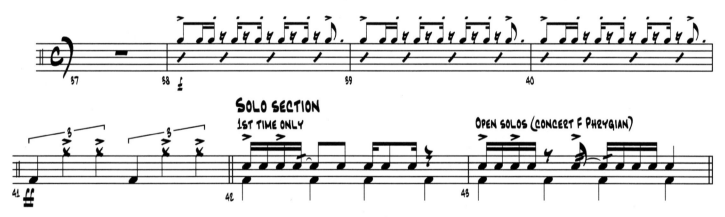

Example 34, Swing Shuffle Track 60

Beginning at m. 55, this example leads from the alto solo phrase to a trumpet solo. This transition is connected by a fill that helps set up an eighth-note ensemble figure on the + of beat 2.

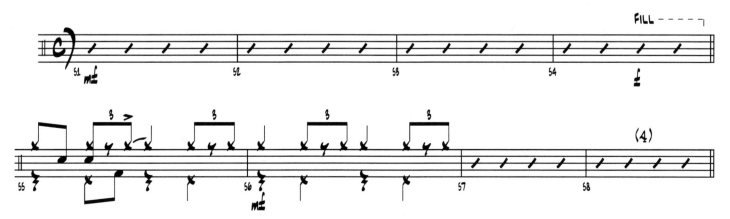

Fill-in-terpretation with Backgrounds

Example 35, Be-Bop Track 61

This phrase toggles between background figures in support of the tenor soloist and full ensemble writing. Eventually, the phrase tapers down dynamically as we arrive at the piano solo. My fill choices rhythmically mirror (for the most part) the written notation played "in the holes" or rests in the phrase.

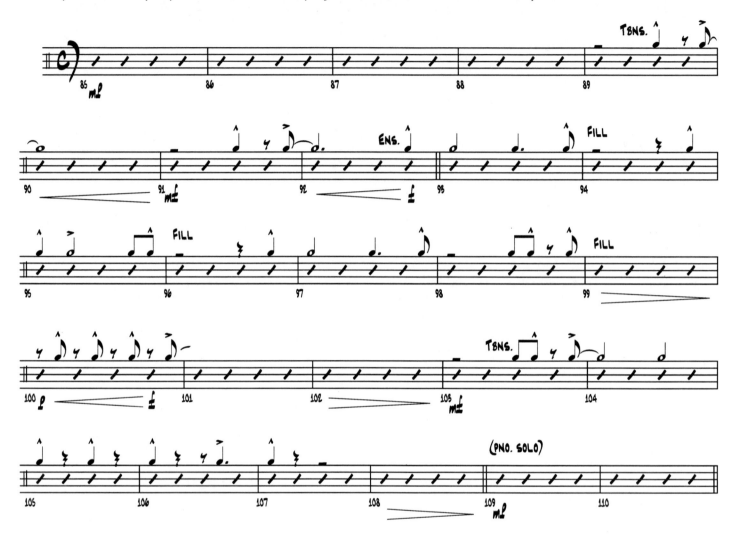

Example 36, Medium Up-Tempo Swing Track 62

In support of the trumpet solo, I uphold the time with brushes and read the written background figures on the bass drum with minimal fills. Notice in mm. 62–63 that I set up the + of beats 2 and 4 on the snare drum by using the exact same rhythm written one beat earlier.

Example 37, Medium Swing Track 63

The following example illustrates an approach to keeping time and stressing the rhythm section background patterns in a looser, more broken feel. Even though it's not written, I play a fill that leads the piano entrance into m. 7.

Example 38, Half-Time Funk Track 64

In support of the trombone solo, I interpret many of the brass and reed background rhythms on the bass drum, while keeping the groove steady and strong. Please note that too much filling in a funk arrangement will detract from the strength and consistency of the pulse.

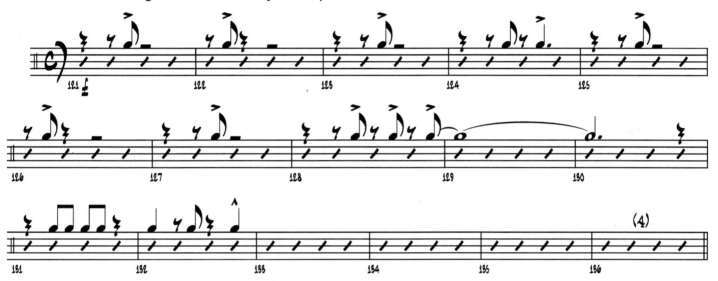

Example 39, Medium Up-Tempo Swing Track 65

This example transitions from one section of the form (solo section) to another (shout chorus). To mark this textural change, I move from brushes to sticks without losing the center of the time feel. As you listen to the MP3 track, notice that as I transition, I keep the hi-hat rhythm consistent on beats 2 and 4 with my foot, so the band has a pulse to lock into. Brushes-to-stick transitions like this are tricky (especially in a recording studio) and take practice. The goal is to make the transition as quickly as possible without dropping a beat (or stick!) The drum fill at the end of the phrase helps to transition to and emphasize a new section of the form.

Shout Chorus Fill-in-terpretation

Example 40, Bright Swing Track 66

The example below is known as a "soft shout chorus" because the entire ensemble is playing, but at a softer dynamic level. Reading the written articulation markings throughout a phrase such as this is key to keeping a crisp time feel for the band. The longer, held note values are opportunities to fill and connect the subsequent phrase.

Example 41, Swing Shuffle Track 67

This phrase helps bring the shout chorus to a close. I set up the *forte* ensemble figures with a fill that's articulated on the crash cymbal, bass drum, and snare drum. To match the dynamic texture (*mezzo forte*) in m. 85, I set up the phrase with a similar fill, but this time by playing the hi-hat. Notice that I play an accent on the + of beat 4 with the crash cymbal and bass drum. I played that rhythm to "signal" to the ensemble that we're almost at m. 87 (in case everyone's attention level wasn't at 100 percent).

Example 42, Jazz March Track 68

This example transitions from a trumpet solo to a twelve-measure ensemble shout chorus, then concludes with a two-measure drum solo march. Each phrase depends on a clear, concise fill to help lead the music from one section of the form to the next. As I played, I tried linking each phrase together with a fill that was clear and purposeful.

Example 43, Medium Up-Tempo Swing Track 69

The following example crescendos from the solo section to the shout chorus portion of the arrangement. Big band drummers help dictate the dynamic shaping for the ensemble, making it important to exaggerate the dynamics as fills bridge each section of the composition together. Once we arrive at the shout chorus (m. 129), notice how each fill adds excitement and intensity to the music.

Ensemble Figures with Drum Solos

Example 44, Latin Track 70

In the example below, each one-measure drum solo, beginning in m. 12, helps "frame" each written ensemble figure. As I sight-read, I used the ensemble-figure rhythms as a springboard to create my own rhythmic improvisations between each ensemble entrance. In m. 13, notice that the eighth notes on beats 1 and 2 "ascend" up the scale. I mirror this shape by playing the figures in unison with the band, ascending from my floor tom to the snare drum.

Example 45, Swing Shuffle Track 71

The drum solo fills I play in this phrase help frame each ensemble entrance. I center my solo ideas around eighth-note triplet patterns with accents, so the band can feel the pulse to ensure clean entrances. To acknowledge the crescendo in m. 104, I play a fill and accent with the band using the bass drum and crash cymbal.

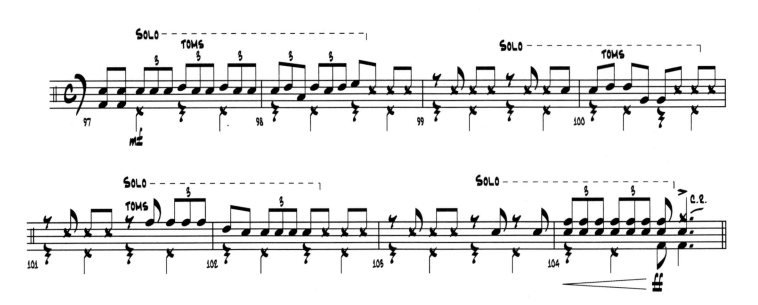

Example 46, Medium Up-Tempo Swing Track 72

This drum-solo phrase is accompanied by "stop time" ensemble figures, so once again my solo treatment had to be rhythmically clear for each band member in the studio. As you listen to the MP3 CD, notice at the end of my solo phrases that I had five beats to transition from sticks back to brushes for the restatement of the melody.

Example 47, Funk Track 73

This seven-measure phrase, beginning at m. 63, leads to one-measure ensemble trades with the drums. As I solo, I'm focusing on each sixteenth-note subdivision, trying to keep each as consistent as possible to allow for clean ensemble entrances between each of my solo statements. Phrases such as this can turn into a musical "train wreck" very quickly if the soloing drummer isn't careful and clear with each improvisation. This section leads back to a restatement of the melody.

Example 48, March-Like Groove Track 74

The example below demonstrates ways of improvising around ensemble figures. At times I use the written figures in my solo statements. I also keep the hi-hat consistent on each quarter note to help the band feel the pulse as I solo. In m. 73, I incorporate the cowbell into the mix to help signal to the band that we're moving on to the next phrase.

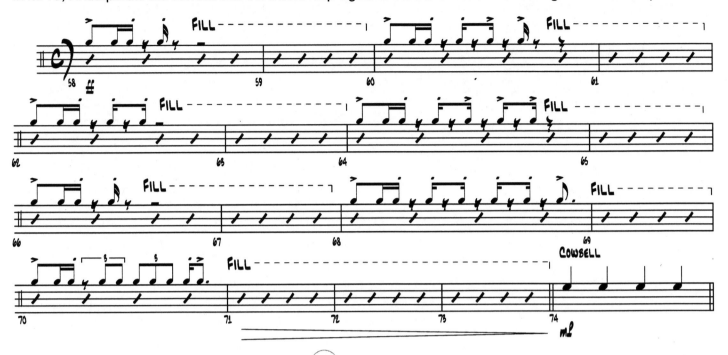

Example 49, Half-Time Funk 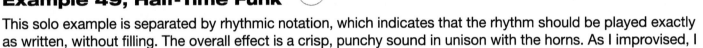 Track 75

This solo example is separated by rhythmic notation, which indicates that the rhythm should be played exactly as written, without filling. The overall effect is a crisp, punchy sound in unison with the horns. As I improvised, I scanned the part and looked ahead to be sure I played the quarter-note triplet rhythm with the band accurately.

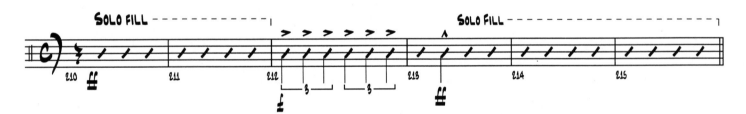

Example 50, Medium Swing 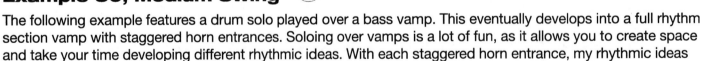 Track 76

The following example features a drum solo played over a bass vamp. This eventually develops into a full rhythm section vamp with staggered horn entrances. Soloing over vamps is a lot of fun, as it allows you to create space and take your time developing different rhythmic ideas. With each staggered horn entrance, my rhythmic ideas get more complex and crescendo with intensity. This phrase leads back to a restatement of the melody.

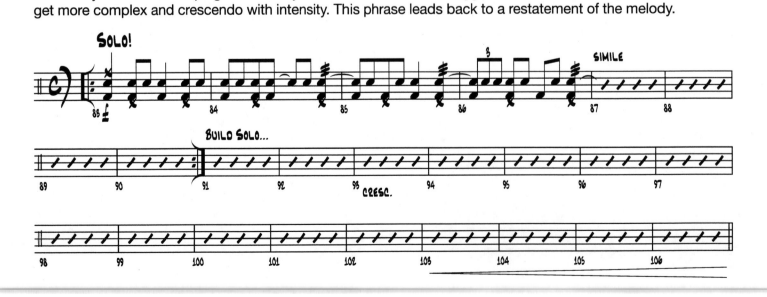

Fill-in-spiration Selected Discography

Buddy Rich:

"Love for Sale," February 22, 1967–March 10, 1967. *Big Swing Face*, Pacific Jazz CDP 7243 8 37989 2 6.
"West Side Story Medley," September 29, 1966–October 10, 1966. *Swingin' New Big Band*, Blue Note 35232.
"Groovin' Hard," March 30, 1970–April 1970. *Keep the Customer Satisfied*, Blue Note 23999.
"Big Swing Face," February 22, 1967–March 10, 1967. *Big Swing Face*, Pacific Jazz CDP 7243 8 37989 2 6.
"Come Back to Me," September 17, 1966. *The Sounds of '66*, DCC Jazz CD DJZ-625.

Mel Lewis with Thad Jones:

"Tiptoe," January 20, 1970–May 25, 1970. *Consummation*, Blue Note BST 84346.
"Central Park North," June 17, 1969 and June 18, 1969. *Central Park North*, Solid State SS-18058.
"Jive Samba," June 17, 1969 and June 18, 1969. *Central Park North*, Solid State SS-18058.
"The Second Race," October 17, 1968. *Monday Night*, Solid State SS-18048.
"Mean What You Say," March 1974. *Live in Tokyo*, Denon Jazz YX-7557-ND.

With Terry Gibbs:

"The Subtle Sermon," March 17, 1959–March 19, 1959. *Terry Gibbs Dream Band, Vol. 1*, Contemporary
    Records CCD-7647-2.
"Cottontail," March 17, 1959–March 19, 1959. *Terry Gibbs Dream Band, Vol. 1*, Contemporary Records
    CCD-7647-2.

Sonny Payne with Count Basie:

"April in Paris," January 4, 1956 and January 5, 1956. *April in Paris*, Verve 5214022.
"Kid from Red Bank," June 24, 1958–July 3, 1958. *Count on the Coast, Vol. 3*, Phontastic 7575.
"Corner Pocket," January 26, 1966–February 1, 1966. *Live at the Sands (before Frank)*, Warner Bros. 45946.
"Shiny Stockings," September 7, 1956. *Basie in London*, Universal Japan 0565157.
"I Can't Stop Loving You," January 26, 1966–February 1, 1966. *Live at the Sands (before Frank)*,
    Warner Bros. 45946.

With Frank Sinatra:

"Come Fly With Me," October 18, 1966–November 18, 1966. *Sinatra at the Sands*, Warner Bros. 46947.
"Pennies from Heaven," October 2, 1962 and October 3, 1962. *Sinatra-Basie: An Historic Musical First*,
    Universal Distribution 2720005.
"I've Got You Under My Skin," October 18, 1966–November 18, 1966. *Sinatra at the Sands*,
    Warner Bros. 46947.

Harold Jones with Count Basie:

"Fun Time," October 1968. *Straight Ahead*, Universal Distribution 5086.
"Basie-Straight Ahead," October 1968. *Straight Ahead*, Universal Distribution 5086.

Louie Bellson:

"Skin Deep," December 7, 1951–August 12, 1952. *Ellington Uptown*, Columbia CK-40836.
"For Europeans Only," 1955. *Skin Deep*, Verve 559 825.
"The Boss," November 9, 1982. *Cool Cool Blue*, Original Jazz Classics/Universal 825.
"Caxton Hall Swing," 1955. *Skin Deep*, Verve 559 825.

Jake Hanna with Woody Herman:
"Caldonia," 1963. *Encore*, Mosaic Select MS-031.
"Blues For J.P.," October 1962. *1963*, Verve/Universal Distribution 5894902.

Ed Soph with Woody Herman:
"La Fiesta," April 9, 1973–April 12, 1973. *Giant Steps*, Original Jazz Classics 344.
"Giant Steps," April 9, 1973–April 12, 1973. *Giant Steps*, Original Jazz Classics 344.

With Clark Terry:
"Modus Operandi," 1976. *Clark Terry's Big B-A-D Band Live at Buddy's Place*, Universe UV 060.

The Taylor/Fidyk Big Band:
"When Johnny Comes Marching Home," November 2, 2005. *Live at Blues Alley*, OA2 Records 22027.
"Anthropology," November 2, 2005. *Live at Blues Alley*, OA2 Records 22027.
"Granada Smoothie," 2003. *A Perfect Match*, Writegroove Music 6824.

Peter Erskine with Stan Kenton:
"No Harmful Slide Effects," February 19, 1973 and February 23, 1973. *Birthday in Britain*, Creative World Records/Creative STD 1065.
"Pete Is a Four-Letter Word" September 26, 1974 and September 27, 1974. *Fire, Fury and Fun*, Creative World Records/Creative STD 1073.

John Von Ohlen with Stan Kenton:
"A Little Minor Booze," 1970. *Live at Redlands University*, Creative World Records STD-1015.
"Tico Tico," 1970. *Live at Redlands University*, Creative World Records STD-1015.

Shelly Manne with Stan Kenton:
"Shelly Manne," October 14, 1951 *Live at Cornell University*, Storyville JUCD 2008.
"Artistry in Percussion," November 19, 1943–December 22, 1947. *The Complete Capitol Studio Recordings of Stan Kenton 1943–1947*, Blue Note 21389.

Jerry McKenzie with Stan Kenton:
"Night at the Golden Nugget," September 21, 1960–December 14, 1961. *Adventures in Blues*, Blue Note 5200892.
"Bernie's Tune," 1959. *Kenton Live from the Las Vegas Tropicana*, Capitol 1460.

Dee Barton with Stan Kenton:

"Aspect," September 24, 1962–September 28, 1962. *Adventures in Time: A Concerto for Orchestra*,
      Blue Note CDP 8554542.

Steve Bohannon with Don Ellis:

"New Horizons,"1967. *Electric Bath*, Columbia/Legacy 65522.

Joe Morello:

"Shortin' Bread," June 6, 1961 and November 13, 1962. *Joe Morello*, Bluebird RCA 9784.
"When Johnny Comes Marching Home," June 6, 1961 and November 13, 1962. *Joe Morello*,
      Bluebird RCA 9784.

Nick Ceroli with Bob Florence:

"Evie," June 15, 1979–June 18, 1979. *Live at Concerts by the Sea*, Discovery 70523.

Sonny Greer with Duke Ellington:

"Ko Ko," November 7, 1940. *The Duke at Fargo 1940: Special 60th Anniversary Edition*, Storyville 8316.

Don Lamond:

"Drums in My Heart," 1962. *Off Beat Percussion*, Command 842.

John Riley with Bob Mintzer:

"I Want to Be Happy," November 20, 1993 and November 21, 1993. *Only in New York*,
      Digital Music Products Dmp 501.
"Oye Como Va," January 4, 1998 and January 5, 1998. *Latin from Manhattan*,
      Digital Music Products/Dmp 523.

Ed Shaughnessy with Doc Severinsen:

"Bugle Call Rag," 1991. *Once More . . . With Feeling!*, Unidisc 2268.

The Clayton-Hamilton Jazz Orchestra:

"Max," May 3, 2000 and May 4, 2000. *Shout Me Out!*, Fable Records/Lightyear 54395.
"Squatty Roo," 2005. *Live at MCG*, MCG Jazz/Manchester Craftsmen's Gld/Manchester Craftsmen's
      Guild MCGJ 1017.

Gregg Bissonette with Maynard Ferguson:

"Fireshaker," May 27, 1983. *Live from San Francisco*, Avenue (Rhino) 71704.
"Coconut Champagne," May 27, 1983. *Live from San Francisco*, Avenue (Rhino) 71704.
"BeBop Buffet," May 27, 1983. *Live from San Francisco*, Avenue (Rhino) 71704.

About the Authors

Jazz drummer, author, and columnist **Steve Fidyk**, has earned national and international acclaim as an artist. He is a member of the U.S. Army Blues Jazz Ensemble, leads his own quintet, The Parlour Project, and freelances with vocalist Maureen McGovern. With McGovern, he has performed throughout the country with orchestras, including The Cincinnati Pops, Spokane Symphony, Nashville Symphony, Plano Symphony Orchestra, Baltimore Symphony Orchestra, Buffalo Philharmonic Orchestra, Richmond Symphony Orchestra, and the Jerry Lewis MDA Telethon Big Band. His discography as a co-leader includes *Big Kids* (U.S. Roots), *A Perfect Match* (Write Groove), and *Live at Blues Alley* (OA2).

A committed educator, Fidyk is currently a member of the Jazz Studies faculty at Temple University and a consultant for Jazz at Lincoln Center's *Essentially Ellington* program. He is the author of *The Drum Set SMART Book, Jazz Drum Set Independence: 3/4, 4/4, and 5/4 Time Signatures, Inside the Big Band Drum Chart,* and *Big Band Drumming at First Sight*, which provides information to help students with their drumset sight-reading skills. His educational discography includes hundreds of big band demo recordings for Belwin/ Alfred Music, as well as contributions to the *Modern Drummer* magazine column *Jazz Drummer's Workshop*. For more information, please visit stevefidyk.com.

Percussionist/composer **Dave Black** received his Bachelor of Music in percussion performance from California State University, Northridge. He has traveled around the world, performing and recording with a wide variety of well-known entertainers and shows.

A prolific composer and arranger, Mr. Black has had more than 60 of his compositions and arrangements published by most of the major music publishers, and many of those have been recorded. He has been the recipient of numerous awards and commissions, including 26 consecutive ASCAP Popular Composer Awards, two Grammy participation/nomination certificates, the Percussive Arts Society President's Industry Award, a *Modern Drummer* Readers Poll award (educational book), a *Drum! Magazine* Drummie! award (educational book), and a certified Gold Record award for the sale of more than 500,000 copies of *Alfred's Drum Method*, Book 1. In addition, many of his compositions have been used as source/background music on numerous TV shows and movies, including the film *Drumline*.

As one of the biggest selling percussion authors in the world, Mr. Black is the author and/or co-author of over 25 books, including *Alfred's Drum Method* (the world's current bestseller) and *Sound Innovations for Concert Band*. He currently serves as Vice President and Editor-in-Chief, School and Church, for Alfred Music.